"Every book Leeana writes instantly becomes my new favorite book."

Myquillyn Smith
author of *The Nesting Place*

"*Begin Again* is a sacred invitation to walk forward in our own lives without shame or regret. Leeana Tankersley's words stir the soul and hold space for anyone who feels stuck, overcome, or undone. I want to give this tender, powerful book to every woman in my life."

Emily P. Freeman
Wall Street Journal bestselling author of *Simply Tuesday*

"*Begin Again* is easily the most beautiful thing I have read all year. Profound and soulful, it is a book that will change everything you believe about releasing hurt and choosing rest. Charming and generous, Leeana is the type of writer who gives words to the things we have trouble saying out loud, and offers gentle wisdom that is both fresh and deep. A unique mixture of raw honesty and expectant hope, *Begin Again* leaves you better in every possible way. This is a book you will want to share with your friends and read multiple times."

Mandy Arioto
president and CEO of MOPS International; author of *Starry Eyed*

"Like many, I'm at a point in my life when family, work, and personal responsibilities shimmy and shove something into every nook and cranny of my day. I power through my schedule until it becomes a straitjacket of sorts, and I wonder why I can't escape the feeling of failure that comes with all the unmet expectations I've placed on myself. If, like me, you've wondered why you never seem to 'arrive' at graduation day of the I-Have-My-Act-Together class, find genuine rest and peace within the pages of Leeana's spectacular book. She wisely shows us that we don't need some kind of magical class or long list of steps to be able to forgive ourselves as we figure things out. We need only to settle into a simple practice known as 'begin again.' *Begin Again* is a solid, hopeful, absolutely *enjoyable* read for any woman who leans toward muscling or pushing her way through every season, albeit crazy or calm. Without a doubt, it is the welcomed space where our exhaustion meets God's inexhaustible grace."

Kristen Strong

author of *Girl Meets Change: Truths to Carry You through Life's Transitions*

"*Begin Again* is inspirational, but it isn't a self-help book. It is a treasury of grace. With humor and wisdom and a poetic voice, Leeana reminds us we are not required to fix ourselves and every day offers countless moments in which we can begin again to receive rest and renewal. Leeana filters Scripture, poetry, and ancient wisdom through the lens of the ordinary extraordinary life she and her family live in an old California house scented with jasmine and sheltered by rustling palm trees. Leeana makes room for us in this place and invites us to join her on a journey that begins again and again, yet carries us forward with each new beginning. Now I know that beginning again is not a sign of failure. We begin again because every day offers some fresh grace blowing in as if through an open window. This book is for every woman wondering how to open that window and how to keep it open."

Christie Purifoy

author of *Roots and Sky: A Journey Home in Four Seasons*

"Leeana's eloquent, yet everyday, honesty will give you both the yearning and courage to begin again, no matter what end you may find yourself at. *Begin Again* is like a rich conversation with a dear, and wise, friend who gently encourages you to open the window of your soul and release all that has stifled you. Leeana's words are brimming with empathy, nourishment, bravery, and an appreciation for the process of change. With each turn of the page I found myself saying, 'Me too.'"

Trina McNeilly

author of *La La Lovely: The Art of Finding Beauty in the Everyday*

Begin Again

Also by Leeana Tankersley

Breathing Room

Brazen

Begin Again

The BRAVE PRACTICE of RELEASING HURT & RECEIVING REST

Leeana Tankersley

Revell

a division of Baker Publishing Group
Grand Rapids, Michigan

© 2018 by Leeana Tankersley

Published by Revell
a division of Baker Publishing Group
PO Box 6287, Grand Rapids, MI 49516-6287
www.revellbooks.com

Printed in the United States of America

ISBN 978-0-8007-2714-7

Library of Congress Cataloging-in-Publication Control Number: 2017055524

Author is represented by Christopher Ferebee, Attorney and Literary Agent, www.christopherferebee.com.

18 19 20 21 22 23 24   7 6 5 4 3 2 1

To Steve

I'll know I've been raised from the dead

    when everything becomes a door—

    every brick wall,

    every dead end,

    every Judas friend,

    everything we see and smell and taste,

    everything we think and feel and are,

    every mountain top and valley bottom,

    every birth and every death,

    every joy and every pain,

    every ecstasy and infidelity,

    when every single thing

    becomes a door

    that opens to eternity

    and we pass through

    as we could never do

    before.

Then we'll wonder why

    we've spent so many years

    just stopping at these doors;

    why we've always pulled up short,

    and turned around,

    and walked away,

    instead of simply

    passing through.[1]

                       Fr. Francis Dorrf

Contents

Foreword

SHAUNA NIEQUIST

One of the best things a writer can do, in my view, is tell the truth about his or her own inner experience in such a way that it makes the reader feel seen and known, included in a universal story. Another way to say it: as a writer, my goal is to whisper to the reader on every page, *"You're not alone, and you're not crazy."*

This book does that. This book is an act of generosity, of hospitality—*sit down here, walk with me through this.*

Leeana and I are busy-minded, anxious, kindred spirits, women who long for bravery and beauty and freedom of soul and spirit . . . and who frequently find their minds to be their own worst enemies. And I suspect that Leeana and I are not the only two women who live in this place—aching for wide, open-souled life, while finding themselves stuck in loops of exertion and exhaustion.

What I'm coming to know, and what Leeana so lovingly offers to us in these pages, is that almost every meaningful part of life comes to health and wholeness through practice, through repetition, through the willingness and humility to begin again. When it all feels stuck, all we can do is begin again.

For those of us who love the prevailing myths of grand gestures and overnight transformation, this is really bad news. Again? Again? Again? I so badly want to be fixed, cured, altered irrevocably.

But the truth resounds, doesn't it, with all we know of life? The best things are built over time. The deepest, most durable, most rooted parts of our souls are not developed in a rush, but in repetition, in beginning again, again, again.

This Benedictine idea of beginning again strikes me as deeply true, and deeply difficult, as most things are. What I do know is that as I disabuse myself of the notion of quick fixes, the idea of beginning again connects with me—a way to hold my heart in position.

My father-in-law is a chiropractor, and one thing I've heard him say to patients over the years is that the real lasting healing is not in the adjustment—the manual realignment of the spine. The lasting healing comes when the muscles that hold the spine are strengthened to the point that they are able to hold the spine in alignment.

There is nothing glamorous about this. Many people would rather have their chiropractor crack them satisfyingly back into shape than strengthen the muscles that will keep them in shape. But as in all of life, the small, ordinary practices are the ones that transform us most completely, that actually change our bodies and souls, that give us new capabilities, new eyes, new hearts.

That's what this book is about: learning to build and nourish our souls through loving repetition—through being humble and brave enough to begin again, again, again.

My favorite books are the ones that give you a sense of the writer—who they are, what they love, what moves them, and what scares them. Leeana is a writer that you begin to know across the pages—I can picture the bougainvillea even while I'm firmly planted in the Midwest as I read. I can smell the salt and see the golden Southern California evening light. I can feel the table and the coffee, the quiet of the mornings.

Through her writing over the years, Leeana has reached deep inside herself and offered her readers her own life and soul with such generosity, and this book is her richest and most generous yet.

● ● ●

Introduction

Restless

Our heart is restless until it finds its rest in thee.

St. Augustine

Nine years ago, I was a brand-new mother to boy/girl twins, and everything felt enormous. My love was enormous. My fear was enormous. My self-contempt was enormous. My exhaustion, enormous. The pile of empty Diet Coke cans, enormous. The babies' beauty, enormous. The weight of how perfect it all was, just waiting for me to mess it up, enormous.

I could not cut a path through the extraordinary landscape. It was all just huge. And so I felt nailed to the couch, floating, in love and entirely anxious. Like I wanted to crawl out of my own skin. Of course, you have no idea what I'm talking about whatsoever.

It was in these very early days of motherhood that I read the line from the Rule of Saint Benedict, which transformed into not just a line but a lifeline and has been with me every day since those winter days almost a decade ago.

Always we begin again.

Benedict's rule for monks called out the holiness of repetition, even the spiritual efficacy of it, though our culture preaches only the opposite. It gave a certain grace to beginnings that saved me over and over again in those days of being a beginner.

Because that's all those days were: one beginning after another. And let's be honest, that's what so much of life is—learning how, and learning how again, over and over. Each day is brand new, after all. We've never lived this day before. It is certainly difficult to not get impatient, even contemptuous, with ourselves over our utter noviceness in life. And the difficulty of being new and inexperienced tempts us to become experts, or in some cases *pretend* we are experts, long before we actually are.

The beginning space was actually a holy space, not just a layover on my way to something better.

So this emphasis on the sacredness of beginning and beginning again was a hold in what felt like vast amounts of thin air. It was permission to be unaccomplished, to be a beginner, to be brand new. More than permission, too, a sense that I was right where I should be and that the beginning space was actually a holy space, not just a layover on my way to something better.

I put the "Always we begin again" sentence in my pocket and have carried it around since. Four simple-enough words have alchemically been both a guide and a companion to me. Even on the heels of the most overwhelming moments, I could begin again. When nothing else helped or made sense, I could always begin again. Just the knowledge that this hand was forever reaching toward me comforted me like little else.

We are a restless breed, we human beings. Our Hard and our Hurts propel us and paralyze us and it's a real trick to recommit to each moment. We spend a lot of restless energy hurling ourselves back into an unchangeable past or forward into an unknowable future.

We want rest. In fact, I think most of us are borderline desperate for rest: a break from all the agitation that enervates our bodies and our minds. We want the capacity to stay right where we are instead of reeling from regret or forecasting. We want peace from the inside out, building a life on something settled and centered inside us, but all this is hard to come by, isn't it. Which is why I believe the practice of beginning again is one of the single most significant gifts you can give yourself.

I want to talk to you about how beginning again helps us live moment to moment, all the while nudging us, gently, on our journey of transformation. Without it, we get stuck. Beginning again invites us out of all the various corners we'd prefer to stay in: safety, swirling, shame, striving, scarcity, shoulds . . . to name a few.

I will pan in and show you myself in my driveway, crazy-eyed and sweaty, invited to begin again. I will pan out and show you myself in my work and my home and my faith, needing a robust dose of courage, invited to begin again. I will cut a cross section of my soul and show you my longings to be naked and unashamed, and my insistence on self-protection, invited to begin again. And I will tell you how I'm just now learning to bring my hurt to God and, in its place, receive rest.

God's story is a narrative of emancipation. Here's the heart of it: What we thought was an ending may very well be a beginning. When the hissing in our ear tells us it's *over*, God whispers an opportunity. *Here's a place we could start from*, he says. *Here's a rock bottom. Hooray. Let's see this for what it is: a possibility.*

And we get the gift of being able to seek resurrection instead of annihilation, even though things might feel so very bleak. How is it possible that this is the start of freedom? I don't know, exactly. But I believe it could be.

Whether you are huddled in your closet right now, hiding from your children, or you are navigating the dissolution of an important relationship, or you are embarking on new work that is requiring more from you than you imagined—whether your life feels impossibly small or overwhelmingly enormous—just think of this book as my way of sliding a note to you on a scrap of paper. When you open it, you will find my message to you:

Breathe and begin again.

• • •

Part I
Too Tight

one

On Opening Up

In returning and rest you shall be saved.

Isaiah 30:15 NKJV

It was late spring and the breeze brought up the jasmine from the gate where it climbs. I walked through the house, room by room, opening doors and windows. Letting air move through the house. Every opened window, every opened door, a prayer.

Come in.
Help.
Thank you.

I opened the entire house. Cranked windows wide open. Found stools and baskets to prop the doors. And then I stood in the very center of our house. I tilted my chin up slightly, and I closed my eyes and let the air move across my face.

We live amidst rolling hills of avocado orchards in Southern California, and our 1930s house is perched on one of those hills, so we almost always have a breeze. But the house had been sealed up, and you couldn't feel any movement at all.

Sometimes a house feels tight, no matter how many square feet it is. Sometimes a heart and a life feel tight. Sometimes a marriage feels tight. Sometimes our work or our calling feel tight. Sometimes the skin we're in feels tight. We need a door or a window to open, a fresh breeze of perspective, the movement of change, but we don't always know how to get there from here.

Opening life up when things feel tight is a vulnerable move. Keeping everything sealed feels so much safer. What will we find when we open the door? What will slide in through all those screens? What is waiting for us behind the windows?

I did not open the house sooner because I had been too afraid of being overwhelmed. I was too afraid of discomfort, hurting. Ancient wisdom tells us the truth will set us free, but sometimes it feels more like the truth will consume us. I have had a couple of distinct seasons in my life when I got overwhelmed, truly, and there seemed to be little I could do about it. For example, there was a time when my brain got scrambled up, and I couldn't unscramble it. And it was really, really hard.

I believed everyone was paying for my scrambled-up brain, and that made it all worse. I have talked and walked and prayed and breathed and written and listened my way through the scramble, but it won't likely ever be gone. And recently, **I began to realize that I** had been ordering parts of my life on the sole basis of avoiding ever being overwhelmed again. When we do this—avoid, especially avoid a low-lying truth—we begin to split off from ourselves, which is why things start to get tight. We see that our ways of being are getting in the way of our being. And, in our attempts to secure space for ourselves, we have somehow walked ourselves into tight.

When this tightness arrives—for any reason—my initial response is to lock, seal, slam, secure, bolt. I shut out. I don't want my imperfections to be witnessed. I don't think I can tolerate that kind of exposure. I do this as a means of self-protection. I do this as a way to control my image as someone who is special.

I avoided until I could no longer avoid anymore, and that's when the gentle voice whispered in my ear, like it had so many times before, *Leeana, always we begin again.*

The word *begin* has rare origins. I like that. It's such a common word in most respects, but its roots are not. Simply put, there aren't many other words like it. One of the root meanings of *begin* is "to cut open" or "to open up."

Geesh. Who wants to do that? Who wants to endure that kind of vulnerability? Emily Dickinson has this curious poem about surgeons being careful when cutting someone open because under the surface is a Culprit. And that Culprit is called Life.

I take that to mean that something living and breathing and flowing is inside each of us. This is both scary and thrilling. We want to let it out. And we are terrified of letting it out. Letting Life out, and therefore, letting Life in, is a risk somehow. On paper, it's such a great idea to open ourselves up. But for some of us, in practice, it's not as easy as we had assumed.

What if I open up and that opening is the very thing that ruins me? I know that when I do, I will cut open a surface that I cannot quickly whipstitch back together. *Oh, never mind. I don't really want to go there, after all.*

Because maybe it's gone badly for us in the past. Maybe we were open and unguarded and we got pummeled somehow—from our outside world or from our inside world. And we have learned that in order to function in this wide world with our particular brain and our particular body, we must be far more vigilant and protective and measured.

Like everything in life, this works . . . until it doesn't.

"You're kind of hard to get to," a friend said to me recently. I was shocked to hear her say that. *No, I'm not,* I thought. *I'm entirely accessible. I'm as open as it gets.* But her words haunted me enough, bothered me enough, to indicate some validity. True, I didn't answer my phone when she called. I don't like talking on the phone. And true, I didn't want to make too many plans or be too available since that would ultimately translate into expectations that I would inevitably not be able to meet. True, I shied away from spontaneous invitations.

I can sit down at a table and tell you the entire contents of my soul, but I also have a constant, buzzing temptation to create distance in the dailiness of life. Even with people I want to share life with. I never want to be a disappointment.

But these strategies wear out. Maintaining calculated distance becomes harder than showing up just as I am. Or, at least, I'm wondering if that's the case. What if trying to keep ourselves safe is the thing that's actually making life feel tight?

I dropped off my friend's son at her house, the same friend who said I was hard to get to. I thought I was just dropping him off, but when I pulled into her driveway, I saw another one of our friends was there too and all the kids were playing. I walked in the house, seized with the desire to offer pleasantries and leave. I had yesterday's eye makeup halfway on and I hadn't prepared myself for conversation.

They invited me to sit, let my kids out of the van and play. And for some reason I could not say yes. While the two of them sat on the kitchen barstools drinking LaCroixs from cold cans, I proceeded to talk with them for twenty minutes while I stood, staring at the chair, trying to decide if I would sit down or not.

What if trying to keep ourselves safe is the thing that's actually making life feel tight?

Finally, after I realized my kids had long since escaped the car and I was enjoying myself, I sat down. But it took twenty minutes.

It takes a lot of energy to stand there in no-man's-land.

Something in me would not flow and could only freeze. Why? Why was I so invested in staying closed? These are women I love, women I have vacationed with, women who love my family. These are women who know me. I had nowhere to be, no plans for the day, no one waiting for me somewhere else. And I could not sit down.

I remember a season in late elementary school to junior high to early high school when I did not feel comfortable eating in public, especially at school. One of my first boyfriends took me to a fancy restaurant and ordered me orange roughy and all I wanted to do was make out instead of eat that fish. Not because I was dying to make out but because I was desperate to avoid eating there at the table while he stared at me.

This stage passed, but I think about it every so often: this young person inside me who is self-conscious, afraid of exposure, putting the brakes on when things get too vulnerable. She wants to be seen and she's scared of being seen.

But what if we don't need to be in a state of self-protection and self-preservation at all times? What if—even though it may be disguised as something else—grace is always lurking behind everything we're trying to keep closed?

I did sit down, with my crazy eyes and my semi-scrambled brain. And when it was time to leave and one of the friends asked me to join her and her kids for lunch, I went to lunch too. I bristled momentarily, and then I made the decision to breathe and open up.

To begin. Right there in that simple little Sunday afternoon moment.

Every time we begin, something in us—even the smallest amount—must open up in the exact place where we want to stay shut. For me, this almost always feels counterintuitive at first. Exposure versus protection? I'll take safety, thank you very much. To be exposed—to be left without shelter or defense—is something to be avoided, not invited.

I've been wondering lately if God's constant invitation, though, is to bring us back to naked and unashamed. And dang if that isn't difficult—to be that exposed, to endure *connection* instead of settling for *contact*.

Exposure, after all, is what lets the light in.

One of the most genuinely inconvenient truths I know is that often something has to die in order for something new to live. And so when we know—deep down—that something isn't working, there's also a part of us that knows what it's going to take to make the thing work again. Likely, it's going to take a death.

Those possible deaths we don't want to face, those ways of being that we're so invested in that we are gripping them with every bit of energy we can muster, lead us to thoughts like these: Don't touch my addiction to work. Don't touch my overeating. Don't look twice at my spending. Do not get close to my resentment. Don't even think about asking me to give up my victim status. Do not, I repeat, do not, come near my codependence.

Jesus himself taught this to his people. He said,

Listen carefully: Unless a grain of wheat is buried in the ground, dead to the world, it is never any more than a grain of wheat. But if it is buried, it sprouts and reproduces itself many times over. In the same way, anyone who holds on to life just as it is destroys that life. But if you let it go, reckless in your love, you'll have it forever, real and eternal.[1]

But who in their right mind wants to look death in the eyes? Or, at least, the possibility of death. It's hard to think about letting something fall apart, only to put it back together again in a different way.

But on the other side of death, the other side of surrender, is this: movement in, space for movement, in the places where things have been locked down, shut down, deeply tight. We can unseal our hearts. Even just a willingness to reach for the window handle and turn it slowly. Feel the cross breeze.

In that allowing, we step into a place that is not yet. Maybe reluctantly. Maybe with the hardest of hearts, but we leave space for the possibility that something fluid and alive is on its way.

I walked through my house. This home that we bought while living in the Middle East for my husband's job. Steve flew to San Diego for thirty-six hours to walk through it with a laptop and Skype and a questionable internet connection so I could "see" it before we closed. The first time I physically walked through it, we already owned it.

This home that we brought two four-year-olds and our new one-year-old to live in, to make a life in. This home with its overgrown wisteria and reaching palms and potted bougainvillea and wild lavender. This home with brick walkways and inlaid Spanish tile and the most finicky plumbing. This home with good bones and a bad backsplash. This home that looks out on the city of El Cajon with the big beige block that was once the El Cajon jail. I grew up just a mile from this home, and when we were little, my mom would take us for kraut dogs and corn dogs and a million tiny packets of yellow mustard and then we'd go to the building site and watch all the diggers and dozers build that jail.

This home.

Beginning again on this day means I will open up—my clenched hands, my heart, my strategies, my life. I walk through this home, into and out of every single room, opening it up to something that is beyond me.

● ● ●

two

Held

You can't force these things.
They only come about through my Spirit.

Zechariah 4:6

I've started getting up at 5 a.m. Not every day, but more days than not. This is an anomaly for me. Normally, I am addicted to sleep. But this pre-twilight pocket, between night and morning, seems like it has something for me. "New life starts in the dark," author Barbara Brown Taylor writes. "Whether it is a seed in the ground, a baby in the womb, or Jesus in the tomb, it starts in the dark."[1] I have a hunch this is true.

So, I get up in the darkness, climb the three steps out of my bedroom, pass through the dining room and turn on the heat as I walk by the thermostat. I walk directly to the coffeepot (obviously) and brew ten cups of coffee. And then I walk to my desk. I have a stack of books and a legal pad next to my laptop on my desk, and everything gets moved over to the kitchen table while I wait for the coffee to brew. There, at the kitchen table, I assemble my nest.

I don't know why I don't just sit down at my desk. I never do. I always walk to the kitchen table, which sits in a nook at the east end of our kitchen. My subconscious mind has not yet been interrupted. Nothing has intruded my senses. Out the windows is only stillness.

I sit and drink black coffee and listen and write. Undistracted. I write on the top of my paper:

God, what do you want to say to me this morning?

And I just listen, keeping track of a dialogue that sometimes arrives quickly and completely and sometimes arrives fragmented and unresolved. I have been asking God this question for a while now, but never in the dark, never early in the morning like this. I'm beginning to believe, though, that there are treasures hidden in the darkness.[2] And when you are beginning a journey of opening up, you need these hidden treasures along the way.

I chose the word *listen* for my word this year. The root means "to honor." I love that.

Sometimes we don't have access to the answers within ourselves. They are there. I believe that. But we just can't get to them. The truth is buried or silenced and we need help to know the next right step.

The poet Rainer Maria Rilke talks about "waiting for faraway things,"[3] the mystery of holding space for something to arrive that we cannot control. Sometimes we're waiting on a miracle. A word.

A whisper. Waiting for the next step to reveal itself. Waiting for a sign. A handle. A hint. For healing. Waiting for peace. Waiting for God to give us this day our daily breadcrumb. Waiting for a yes. Waiting for a no. Waiting for any answer.

I am waiting for some answers—how am I to alleviate some of these tight places in my life? What is the plan, God? What is the way ahead? How and when am I to open up?

Rilke's emphasis on this waiting is that it's frustrating. (No kidding.) It's frustrating to be patient—with God, with ourselves, with the process—and wait for the mysterious unfolding. Waiting on something "Other" is not easy work. But we cannot force these things, as the prophets and the monks and the mystics all tell us. We aren't the ones in control.

We tried that, being in control, and here we are, listening in the dark.

The decision to get up early starts the night before. Around 7 p.m., I begin to feel the hum of anticipation. I'm anticipating that first sip of coffee the next morning, the quiet house, the ritual of turning on the heat, lighting a candle, wrapping up in a blanket. I'm anticipating getting ahead of the day, instead of running to catch up with it. I'm anticipating the way it feels to start the day with a practice instead of a panic. Practices invite us to submit our own agenda and energy, and this kind of submission to what's good for me—like exercise or drinking water—is satisfying. By 8:30 p.m. I'm in bed.

"Listening is something you never regret," I recently heard acoustic ecologist Gordon Hempton say.[4] I think that's true. And with more voices than ever bombarding us, vying for our attention and soul space, I could just as easily grab for a solution in the din. That would be quicker, my frantic self tells me. Ingest some information.

A low knowing inside me hints to me that the noise is not where I will find my guidance. I will be led by listening to the silence. Listening *into* the silence.

Listening is about trading our trying for trust. This is how we find true rest, I believe. Listening is a begin-again kind of ritual. It's never finished and it's always possible, and it's waiting to give us living and breathing gifts that are new every morning. We start where we are, not where we want to be, which requires a new level of honesty with ourselves.

We start where we are, not where we want to be, which requires a new level of honesty with ourselves.

We sit at the kitchen table, God and I. And for those ninety minutes, I repeatedly have a sense that I am joining a practice that is ancient, and yet I stand on new ground. I am lost in a sacred world. And yet I am returning home. The inky curtain on the other side of the windows covers any trace of life. My feet are firmly planted *here*, but I am waiting on something from *there*.

Caught.

I have never liked the idea of being caught. Between two people. Between warring entities of any kind—ideologies, theologies. Caught between that little girl inside me who feels fragile and weak and needy and the warrior woman inside me who feels ready and resilient.

I felt caught as a child, which was a by-product of divorce. A child just feels caught. Pretty much no matter what, I think. Because they are imprinted with a desire for wholeness, and when that wholeness is fractured, they are left a bit confused. Adults have the capacity to navigate this—kinda—but children really don't. And so a skin, a tough skin, gets layered over the child's openness, and the message is, "Don't you dare get caught again. Getting caught is a lose-lose. Don't ever be *between* again."

This makes us distrust any kind of middle. We have lost control and we are dependent on the process pulling us through, like a gravitational field. But it's hard to trust. Because, it seems, being dependent on a process has only ever been a problem in our young past.

I do not like being caught between my own needs and others', and so I have shut myself down at times, afraid of what leaning into issues will cost me. This is the freaked-out, codependent nine-year-old inside me, but I don't realize that. At least not yet. Her needs are preeminent because she squawks the loudest. She cannot deal with any more discomfort, and so when she thinks I'm on a one-way train to *caught*, she is always quick to remind me that I will lose.

My caughtness is no coincidence, of course. God is going to agitate me and see if I am ready to begin again or not. It's OK if I'm not ready. There will be other opportunities. But if I am ready or at least willing to be ready, I might just as well stand in the center of this holy tension.

Holy tension is something we either explore or ignore. We get to choose. But let's not be fooled: both exploring and ignoring have consequences. And perhaps, now at age forty-two, I am ready to decide which choice carries a greater cost.

While it doesn't immediately feel this way, I'm beginning to wonder if this tension is actually a chance to come home. But—and this is a big but—in order to come home, we will have to walk the very road we think will undo us.

I am at the point in the hero's journey that is known as "the wall." I will see the wall as a door, or I will come to it and see it as a wall and turn and walk away. Whatever my response—resentment, contempt, blame-shifting, fear, hope, possibility, trust that I have been brought to this wall for a reason—will reflect my seeing. Door or wall.

If I walk away, it's OK. It means I am not ready. And God will wait. If I choose to open the door, I am choosing innumerable beginnings. I am choosing the opening up.

A silvery-slivery moon still sits in the sky. I'm listening to an old song on repeat. It's about God's light shining on us.

We don't have to do any of this, of course. We do not have to wait, hands open, in the dark. This is not mandatory. But there will come a time when we know, in a place that does not have words, that our strategies are exhausted and what we are working and pressing and striving for still hasn't arrived. And we admit we want something—rest—that we cannot secure for ourselves.

I'm reminded there is another kind of caught. Not just the one that means "trapped." The word can mean something different altogether: "held." As in, I was falling, and Someone caught me.

I am not only caught between dark and light, caught between where I am (tight) and where I want to be (rest), I am also mysteriously held. I'm convinced, through this 5 a.m. ritual, that if nothing else, I am held—benevolently—and my job is to give in to this held-ness instead of trying to squirm away because I've got to go prove how worthy I am. I am held. For no other reason than Love.

If I can sit in this truth, that I am held by Love no matter what, I can and will begin again. This is what today's 5 a.m. session offers

34

me. No big plan. Just the simple yet profound knowledge of my held-ness. No matter what, God is holding me.

He says: *You do not need to do more, fix yourself, or hold anything together. You just need to fall back into my grace, trade your trying for trust. Where you are broken and bruised is exactly the place, not in spite of that place, that I want to show you you're beautiful.*

God invites me to "seal in" this work, my listening, my trust, my held-ness. He says, *Breathe and begin again. Keep coming to the table and I will keep showing you the way.*

Seal it in your heart and your body, he invites. Lock it in so that you don't forget.

I see the sun rise from my seat in the kitchen. Ahhhh, maybe this is why I am magnetically drawn to the east end of the house. I know it is where I will see the first hints of dawn.

I walk outside, look at the metallic morning sky. I look up and out over the trees, light now breaking through a cloud-mottled sky, turning twilight into today. I have sat waiting for faraway things. My daily breadcrumb arrives: I am held. I swallow it down with my black coffee. Communion.

I head back in and start bacon in the cast-iron skillet. Any minute, kids will stagger in, looking for hugs and snuggles. Luke will find me at the kitchen table and burrow into my side and his buzz cut will prickle the bottom of my chin. I will have the slightest sense of spaciousness in my chest when I reach toward each of them, one by one, as they emerge.

Let this be a sign unto you.

• • •

three

Donations for Those Less Fortunate

stop believing

in

what hurts you.

Nayyirah Waheed

Even as I wait for faraway things, I must attend to what is right in front of me. Namely, a home and three kids, and all the flotsam and jetsam that comes in the door behind them every day. Requests, solicitations, invitations, forms . . . these tend not to be my forte.

Many of you have file folders and label makers and hooks and systems. I do not speak this language. And so I was particularly impressed with myself when a form came home with the kids asking for donations to the school food pantry, and I felt compelled and able to participate.

I immediately—as not to lose my train of thought or my re-solve—bagged up pantry items we weren't using or could manage without. You know how you go to Costco and see two large jars of pickled beets for $6 and you think, "Hey, pickled beets, I could really do something with those." But then after you have worked your way through the first oversized jar, no one in your household can stand to look at another pickled beet, and the second jar remains, taunting you from the pantry.

I put the second jar of pickled beets in the donation bag. I also found two boxes of tomato basil soup, a can of madras sauce, hominy, and some granola bars. I felt really proud of how this was all going.

As soon as I had two bags full of donations, I yelled to the kids to get their shoes on and head down to the van to go drop off the food items at school. I had a "friend" who let donations to Goodwill sit in the back of her car for, like, almost a year, and I didn't want to be like my "friend," so I told the kids we would go right then and get this little good deed completed.

The kids got their shoes on and I began to herd the cats, herd the cats, herd the cats down to the driveway. I put the bags down, and as I was reaching to open the back of the van, a child screamed from the house as if her arm had spontaneously detached. I ran to the house, found the child and the arm, reattached the arm, and now the other two were back in the house, wanting to see what all the blood and gore was about.

So, again, I began to herd the cats, herd the cats, herd the cats back down to the van. Finally, everyone is buckled and we are on our way! I put the van in reverse, and as I back out, the vehicle makes a strange lurch.

"What in the world was that?" I ask.

"I think it was a ball, Mommy. I saw a ball in the driveway earlier today. You must have run over it," Luke offers.

So I put the car in drive and pull forward so I can unlodge the ball from my tire. But wouldn't you know, the van makes that same strange lurch.

"Man, that's a really resilient ball," I say to the kids. "I'm going to have to hop out and get it."

I walk around the van in order to deal with that pesky ball, and I discover something in absolute horror.

There, spewed across my entire driveway, are pickled beets, tomato basil soup, hominy, madras sauce. A huge pinky-red vomitous smear, as though the world's biggest giant has just barfed in my driveway.

The car window goes down. "Hey, Mom, did you get the ball?" Lane asks.

"Um, no, honey. It wasn't a ball after all," I say.

"Oh, what was it then?"

"Mommy ran over the food donations," I tell her in the quietest voice possible.

Lane looks at me, injured. "Why would you do that, Mommy? Why would you run over the donations for those less fortunate?"

Her voice cracks as she asks, adding the perfect amount of drama to her contempt.

"Did Mom get the ball?" Luke calls to Lane from the back seat.

"No, Luke. Mommy ran over the donations for those less fortunate."

"Why?" Luke's voice quivers. "Why would she do that?"

It's one of those East County San Diego mornings that's in the high eighties and it's not yet 8 a.m. My shirt is now sticking to my back and my internal monologue is not Christlike and my anger begins to roll.

If only Steve weren't on a trip, I wouldn't have to be taking care of all this by myself, and I wouldn't have run over the donations for those less fortunate.

If only one of the kids' arms hadn't spontaneously detached, I wouldn't have been distracted, and I wouldn't have run over the donations for those less fortunate.

If only Honda hadn't installed a subpar back-up camera in this minivan, I would have actually seen what was behind me, and I wouldn't have run over the donations for those less fortunate.

If only the California public school system wasn't trying to sabotage every mother in our county, I wouldn't have run over the donations for those less fortunate.

And then, inevitably I turn on myself and the narrative gets toxic quick:

If only I wasn't so scattered all the time, I'd be one of the moms who is organized and on top of things. One of those moms who doesn't roll over the donations for those less fortunate with her minivan, FOR CRYING OUT LOUD.

If only I was like Cynthia down the street who has great legs, seventeen children under three, and is chairing the food drive single-handedly while wearing at least two of her children at all times, then I'd be putting a beautiful picture of my kids being philanthropic on Instagram instead of staring at this massacre.

There I am, standing in my driveway, getting sucker-punched by Soul Bullies who are giving me more and more ammunition to use against myself, all while I'm ankle deep in chunky beet juice. Man, life is no joke.

The ordinary bumps right up against the extraordinary. Constantly. And, tending to the ordinary while walking through the extraordinary requires so much energy. So much, in fact, that I am often tempted to just shut down.

Immobilized in my driveway, staring down at pantry roadkill, I need a small step in the right direction, but I am glued to the ground, stuck in my corner of self-contempt and rage. I want to give up. On everything. I want to sit down and eat tomato basil soup off the driveway. I'm on a one-way train to Crazy Town.

There's a tap on my shoulder. It's an old familiar monk visiting me. He's got kind eyes and something in his hand. He's handing me a small piece of paper. On it are the words, "Always we begin again."

"You've got the wrong gal," I tell him. I feel entitled to my self-pity and my shame. I want to sit a little longer in this soup. I'm not ready for a way out.

"Leeana, what if we try and begin again? What if we take a deep breath and let some space in to start over? What if we just try?"

My eyes sting as I hear muffled sobs from the despondent children in the minivan.

I am sure it's a doomed strategy. How could any plan possibly hold up to running over the donations for those less fortunate?

You will wake up one morning with absolutely every good intention. You will be armed with momentum and desire and you will have spent some time listening to God. You will feel centered and rooted and you will feel connected to God and to your own soul, but that will not protect you from yourself entirely. And it certainly won't protect you from your children. Your serenity will never insulate you from the chaos that is always lurking.

This is how we come to learn, in the absolute trenches, the power of the words "begin" and "again" right up next to each other. We will need them thirty times in the next ten minutes, maybe more. This is how we hang in there, present and accounted for, in our own lives. We open up, again, when all we want to do is slam shut.

We'd rather resent our partner, badger our children, and forget the less fortunate. In fact, we feel entitled to that posture. At least I do. I should be allowed to nurture my justifiable malice. The only problem is, all this spite does is rot the inside of me.

I have learned enough to know that I might try to believe in that gentle Voice tapping me on the shoulder. I might just try to grasp that hand reaching toward me. It will be there waiting for me when I'm ready.

Beginning again is both a big concept and a very small one. To "begin again" implies a starting over, which feels all-encompassing, a giant task. A blank page, a new job, an unfamiliar city, a fledgling relationship. Beginning again is also the act of taking one small step in the revealed direction, and in that way, it's a micro-movement.

But doesn't being a beginner, over and over, just basically feel like being a failure, like we're never really going anywhere?

The only thing I can say is that for the past decade, as I have held this sacred sentence, "Always we begin again," God has breathed new life into it and made it mean new things in new seasons of my life.

To begin again in my early thirties and in my early days of mothering meant learning to treat myself as I would a friend instead of an enemy. It meant nurturing an entirely new relationship with myself, one that was marked with compassion instead of contempt.

I felt unfit. Not only as a mother but as a person, and this is one of the heaviest weights we can bear. Sure, life was overwhelming in so many ways, but the most overwhelming thing I was experiencing was happening on the inside of me, not on the outside. I did not know how to summon compassion for myself. And this created so much inner tension that I could feel it in my body. Literally in my bones. Circumstances can be challenging, but the most challenging thing I know is when we are not on our own team.

I felt soul-wringing, not only hand-wringing, when I would come up against a decision. I felt convinced that everyone else knew better than I did, and I also felt convinced that there was a strong, knowing voice inside of me, but I couldn't get to her. I had lost her somehow. And I had no idea how to wake her up or jolt her or rally her. I had no idea how to get her back in the game. She, my strong self, had gone dormant. The weakest, most wounded part of me was front and center, needing attention and grace.

And so in the beginning, I was to learn to hold space for myself, to be on my own team, to—truly—learn to tolerate my own holy/holey humanity. I would need this practice, this truth, for the rest of the journey. I didn't totally understand this at the time, but I see now that if we are punishing ourselves, bullying ourselves, beating ourselves up, then there is nowhere to go. We are locked in a self-versus-self battle that does not relent. There is nothing generative about this battle. It is only, always destructive.

"Begin again" became my counterspell to shame. Shame—living out of the belief that I am essentially flawed—casts a paralyzing spell on us. It's ugly and accusing, and it's an epidemic. *You're done*, it says, hypnotizing me every time. But beginning again was a way I could reverse the spell shame had me under.

When we moved our two two-and-a-half-year-olds to Bahrain and I was pregnant with our third and it was Ramadan and 130 degrees and the Sunni and the Shi'a were at each others' throats and there was tear gas and tire fires and rubber bullets and riot police, I had to do something other than beat myself up.

I learned, during that season, that sometimes there is just very little in life we can control. But one thing we can always control is how we treat ourselves. And that one thing can change everything.

Threaded throughout this chaos were gorgeous rugs and generous new friends and garlicky hummus and biryani rice and the most memorable parties. A tiny Ethiopian nanny who saved me. And a bitty baby—all ten pounds of her—who has brought us the most unspeakable joy.

In those days, beginning again meant learning and then remembering that things are mostly hard because they're hard, not because I was failing at life.

And so those early and mid thirties were about forging a new relationship with myself, one decision at a time. One breadcrumb at a time. Sometimes this looked like getting myself the help I needed. Often it meant having the discipline to dialogue with myself as I would a dear friend instead of an enemy.

We returned home to San Diego with our three babies and our buzzing bodies and brains and we needed to recover. So beginning again meant total patience. Waiting, yet again, for a faraway thing to arrive: reorientation after reentry. It all took longer than expected or desired. Doesn't it always?

To begin again in my late thirties was to go in search of myself. This would have been impossible had I never started unraveling the adversarial relationship I had with myself. Because, again, there is no growth in punishment. We cannot demean ourselves into new territory. The source, the motivation, must come from something deeper. A deeper belief that we do not deserve to keep hurting ourselves. A deeper belief that we were made for more. A deeper belief that we want to be well. A deeper belief in God's call on our lives.

So I kept watch for her, and I listened for her voice, and I took notes for her, and followed clues to her: the brazen, without-shame Me. And isn't it interesting that when you begin to recover these beautiful and sacred parts of yourself that have gone dormant for a season, when you begin to wake them up, you also begin to expose the lies you had believed about yourself.

Now, at forty-two, beginning again feels new all over again. Deeper and more surgical than it ever has. Beginning again has attached itself to the most vulnerable places in my life, the most fragile parts of my ego, the deepest places in my story. So, while beginning again might feel cyclical instead of advancing, what we pick up on each turn is the very thing we needed for the next leg of the journey.

There, on my vomitous driveway, I take a deep breath. And then another. All the way in. All the way out. Slow everything down. I just need to reach my hand up and take the grace that is extended toward me. This is hard to do, especially because I feel like I deserve to be sitting in spilled soup. I deserve to drown in this void.[1] The cold ground is where I belong. It's low and familiar. I hate how inept I can be.

I reluctantly take what this gentle monk is handing me. I receive the mercy of a next, new moment. I fall open when what I want to do is slam shut because I've learned—the hard way—that self-loathing will never help me into the next moment.

I move my feet and the puddle I'm standing in sloshes against the soles of my shoes. It's OK. I'm OK. Some days we run over things. Today was my day. Today, I am the less fortunate and, in the end, the donation was for me.

● ● ●

four

Scared-Sacred

Because of the LORD's great love we are not consumed,
for his compassions never fail.
They are new every morning;
great is your faithfulness.

Lamentations 3:22–23 NIV

I'm not sure anyone likes the feeling of too-tight. The agitation is uncomfortable and, at times, painful. We don't want to face it. At least, I don't. If you're anything like me, your first instinct is to numb the agitation.

I am an A#1 Numb-er. Love it. I've used purchasing, alcohol, Netflix, CandyCrush, and Diet Cokes. I've used rolled tacos, Instagram, napping, and Doritos. All of which felt amazing for the moment. I, at any given time, can feel like I'm made up of nothing but nerves, and I want it to all go away. I suffer regularly from

Empathy Hangovers. Sometimes it's all just too much, and it feels good not to feel.

But if I am to be true to beginning again, I need to be a bit more awake to the agitation instead of immediately trying to kick it out. This is clear and also hideous news. Who wants to be awake? I mean, we say we do, but awake is vulnerable and exposed and perhaps more honest than I can tolerate.

But what I began to realize in my 5 a.m. listening is that I was to stop running from discomfort.

I spent a season going to a 12-step group that helped me navigate my emotional life. We, the few of us that attended regularly, circled up our five-or-so chairs in a smoke-scented classroom and we talked about how our inner worlds had become unmanageable. Some people cried. Some people twitched. Some people shook. It was all completely fine, totally normal. Come as you are.

Very quickly into those meetings I learned the upside-down wisdom of taking back our strength by acknowledging our powerlessness. It's absolutely too easy to hide our weakness, compensate for it, even act like it doesn't exist, and try to show the world the slickest version of ourselves. Many of the tribes we belong to celebrate those of us who can consistently keep ourselves in life's great Gifted and Talented program, and we can quickly and easily begin to believe that our slickness—our giftedness and talents—is what makes us interesting and worthy.

Through the wisdom of 12-step, I've learned what it means to walk into a room with other people who have come to the end of themselves and were there to talk about it.

People drove themselves to a room with fluorescent lighting and lukewarm coffee to confess, to say, "I'm ready to admit I can no longer muscle my way through life or numb my way through life or deny my way through life. I need help. I need to start from a place of *honesty* instead of *hiding.*"

At these meetings, of all places, I learned more of what it meant to begin again—to watch people decide they no longer deserved to keep hurting themselves and see them regain strength right there in the admission of their weakness.

Do you see how this is so subversive? In our weakness, we become strong. It is only in our refusal to look at our weakness that we remain weak, because all that unexamined tightness has more than enough energy to keep us miserably stuck.

The most beautiful part of it was the honesty, the willingness to sit in the true state of affairs without needing to pretend something else was going on. And this wasn't for the sake of others, for appearances. Truly, when people spoke and told their stories, you got the sense that they had crashed through every last layer of pleasing, posturing, and performing. They were sitting in that room, building a new foundation that had nothing to do with the ego. The ego was no longer in charge.

A death had occurred, the death that always must take place if the hero's journey is to continue. And now they were ready to live out of something totally new:

Striving was exchanged for surrender.

I understand that this sounds romantic and spiritual and lovely in theory. And I also know, for an absolute fact, that this is gnarly and life-altering and just shy of practically impossible in practice. Let's not pretend this isn't hard. It is just so much easier to cover, compensate, and control than to look right at the discomfort. And let me be clear, I don't think God blames us for looking the other way, but I also think God's in the business of coaxing us toward wholeness.

At the 12-step meetings you could feel the surrender, palpably, in the room. Nobody could muster the energy to pretend anymore. Brutal honesty was going to be the only path to sobriety, come what may.

I am deeply longing for an undivided, honest life. One that is free from image maintenance and façading. One that doesn't require covering up and explaining away. And I don't just want to be honest with everyone else. I'm longing to be honest with myself. And I am also aware that I have to surrender in order to let God heal the divisions.

Did you know the word *Sabbath* translates "to stop"? Sometimes beginning again is actually about stopping instead of starting.

Where there is pretending, stop.

Where there is overcompensating, stop.

Where there is denial, stop.

Just sit and feel the agitation.

I've been too scared to do this, previously. Now, I am ready. I try to remind myself that the words *scared* and *sacred* are practically identical on first glance. Could the very fact that I'm scared be an indication I'm happening onto something sacred?

49

I'm learning to pay attention to the agitation instead of turning it away. To stop and look at it instead of trying to numb it or escape it. Because, *the invitation is sitting right there in the agitation.*

I sit at the kitchen table and spend fifteen seconds with my eyes closed, scanning my body for tension. Starting at the tip-top of my head and moving down my body all the way to the soles of my feet, I search for tension. You would be surprised how unaware you are of pain in your body until you take the time to acknowledge it.

The invitation is sitting right there in the agitation.

First, I realize my shoulders are, like, up to my ears. Poised and ready for fight or flight. When I drop them and breathe into them, I feel how my neck, shoulders, and back are all burning. Tight, tense, overtaxed. I try to take deep breaths *into* that tightness, expanding the areas that are collapsed and rigid. And it hurts. It actually, physically hurts.

Isn't this fascinating. Our bodies know. They are holding the story—the story of working so hard to hold it all together, of carrying the burden of making everything work, of constructing a no-cracks façade to our work, marriages, families, homes, meals, outfits, health, bodies. At least that's what we think we're doing. It's an impossible burden because of how over-responsible it is. We are heaping the burden of "everything is fine" on ourselves. And in this attempt to keep it all together, we are actually preventing the thing that needs to happen most: the falling apart. The stopping, the Sabbath. The letting go of fine and the letting in of Love.

Most of us, though, would far rather hang on to a known, even if what is known isn't working, even if it requires no faith at all, than venture into the unknown.

Here's what's scared-sacred: We go into death with no guarantee of resuscitation. We'd rather hold on to something that's not working, because at least we're still holding on to something. Letting go, entirely, means that we may be left empty-handed. And that, for most of us, is too uncertain of a reality.

Then, miraculously (and I mean this word literally), we are invited to plunge toward death. (Wow, lucky us.) And this is a kind of awakening. The awakening is a grace. But that doesn't mean the entire process feels good. Sometimes grace grabs you by the jugular.

We begin to feel something leaning on us from the inside. Not the old feelings of shame or condemnation. We can be sure those are not from God. Another word for this is *revelation*. Something is being revealed to us. It is all grace. We can start running like a dog is chasing us, and likely at first we will. But then we will begin to realize that the invitation being offered us is coming from Love, is offered in our best interest, will satisfy our deepest desires. *The agitation holds the invitation*, and it's actually what we've always wanted.

Less trying. More trusting.

Less striving. More surrender.

We get to drop our shoulders and let the crash happen. Death may be the only door to life. God's invitation is to take us further up and further in, to show us how and where and in what direction we could begin again. But we choose. We are not forced into anything.

We can try to hold it all together, or we can open our hands.

● ● ●

five

You Are the One You Have Been Waiting For

Wrestling I will not let Thee go
Till I Thy name, Thy nature know . . .
Speak, or Thou never hence shalt move,
Tell me if Thy name is Love.

Charles Wesley

There's an ancient story about a man named Jacob who wrestled an angel. Jacob and the angel wrestled through the night, as the story goes, and the angel could not beat Jacob. Finally, the angel touched Jacob's hip, dislocating it, in order to try to escape his hold.

Still Jacob refused to let go until the angel had blessed him. Imagine, clutching to a messenger of God and demanding a blessing. The angel acquiesced and gave Jacob a new name: Israel, which means God-wrestler. Finally Jacob let him go. But Jacob never walked the same after this encounter. From then on, he limped.

I love this image. Jacob refusing to unhand an angel of God until he gets what he wants, what he needs. This story tells us that if we need to grab onto God, and make demands of him, we can. We get to wrestle.

Jacob demands to know, Who are you and who am I? Isn't this what we're all asking of God when we get right down to it? Tell me who you are and tell me who I am. "Tell me," Charles Wesley wrote, "if Thy name is Love."[1] Prove it. I will not let you go until I know.

Look me in the eye and tell me if you are really Love. Are you on my team or not?

Steve and I had a very difficult conversation recently, the kind of conversation you don't really want to find yourself in, the kind that Hurts. We sat at the dining room table looking at each other for a long time. I said, "What happens next?" and he said, "One of us will get up in the morning and make the coffee." And that's what we committed to: one of us getting up the next morning and making the coffee. Because some of the time, we can't see past the very next step, the very next beginning. That's all we get.

I want to shake God for this. And he lets me. He would rather I engage than escape, rather I wrestle than numb. That's the lesson of Jacob: the limp is not a mark of failure; it is the mark of showing up.

Showing up and staying in the clench requires infinite recommitments to beginning. Coming back to our conversation with God, speaking our anger or our frustration or our longing . . . again . . . even when we think it will yield nothing.

We don't give up. We keep coming to him. Because we are the only ones who can wrestle this out with God. There are no proxies. In the case of our own lives, "we are the ones we have been waiting for," to borrow a beautiful line from poet-activist June Jordan.[2]

When tension begins to build, I can be the kind of person who is scanning the horizon, looking for someone else to come and take care of things for me. A worthy savior. And I'm not the only one. Case in point: I was having coffee with a friend the other day and she was telling me about a season in her life when she was completely stuck in a too-tight situation, paralyzed.

"So what was holding you back?" I asked.

"I was waiting for someone to come tell me what my rights were."

No one is coming to save you, a voice says to me in the darkness of dawn. *No one is coming to rescue you.* It was God's voice, though it didn't feel like it at first. At first it felt like how Jacob must have felt—like God was working directly against me. Like the very thing I needed was, now, never going to happen. And these words also felt like they were speaking to a gash that resided in the core of me, a gash that would need to be tended.

The Voice that brought me this news was gentle and calm, not a taunt or a bully. And so I listened. But I wasn't happy about it. I wrestled back, angry and hurt. I wanted the cup to pass and I didn't want to have to face life and adult my way through it. I didn't want any more transformation; I wanted to put my head in the sand.

The Voice kept on. *No one is coming. No one is coming. No one is coming. Except you.* It went on . . . *You have the opportunity to give yourself a gift that no one else can give you. You have the opportunity to take yourself by the hand and walk with yourself through this.*

When you have spent seasons overwhelmed, paralyzed, unsure, and holding back—letting your traumatized nine-year-old self be in charge—it is somewhat revolutionary to have someone whisper in your ear, *You can do this. You really can. Everything you need to step forward, you already have. And I am with you.*

As much as I hated to admit it, the Voice was right. Part of the tightness I had experienced was a distrust in my own knowing, my own intuition, my own strength—which had gone offline for a season, up and disappeared.

> **Everything you need to step forward, you already have.**

I have a strange relationship with "knowing." I want *to know*, because this seems strong and smart, but I don't always *know*. In the gap between what I want to know but don't yet, I often believe everyone else has it figured out. One of my most paralyzing Soul Bullies will tell me, "Everyone knows better about you than you."

This is one of the ways I get crippled from the inside out. That Soul Bully is always reiterating: "You are a person who can't possibly know." In other words, I am someone who cannot really be trusted with my own perceptions in a situation. As a result, I've distrusted myself and my experience of things. Even dismissed my own intuition at times as being misguided. And this is one reason I have wanted someone else to come and tell me what my rights are, tell me how to do my life, tell me which direction to go. I want someone else to validate my perception and my plan of action because, after all, I am not a reliable observer in my own life.

55

But, more than anything, I have wanted to know. And I have wanted to appear that I know. And so I've chased knowing, I think. Likely because I didn't want to face the fear that, deep down, I'm afraid I don't know.

As a result, I have listened to unqualified and unsympathetic advisors, believing they knew better instead of sitting still and listening for myself. I have taken the pulse of others without taking my own or without stopping to listen to God's heartbeat.

Recently I facilitated a workshop for a group of women, and 99 percent of the women in attendance hugged me and thanked me on the way out the door, full of love and gratitude for a beautiful morning together. But do you think I could even remember the state of the 99 percent after I talked to the last attendee, the one who critically questioned the content I presented? No, in fact, over the course of a seven-minute conversation, all good feelings about the morning were erased. As she asked me questions, including phrases like "your stance" and "your philosophy," I felt hot and defensive and cornered and very young.

After the event, I rode home with my dear friend Elaine and anxiously recalled to her the woman's concern over my content. Elaine could easily read my insecurity and she finally said to me, "And why do you think she knows better than you do?"

Ummm.

What's most important is to remember that each and every one of us is an eligible receiver. I am eligible to receive wisdom, illumination, comfort, and counsel. These are not things I must wait for others to provide for me. These are things I can receive from God.

Yes, we need others. We need guides and companions. We need people to raise important points of contention. Without question. And we also need to learn the sound of God's voice and the sound of our own voice.

Instead, we heap flesh on top of our liabilities. Once in a while we are graciously led into the depths of our humanity, the holy depths of our humanness, and—if you are like me—it's almost too much to tolerate. In this way, failure, limits, coming to the end of ourselves is all grace, inviting us to let go of our striving ways, our sense that we have to prove we are worthy of taking a seat at the table. Look, I belong here! See all I'm contributing! See how much I'm needed!

But then we see, when we stop running and get still, that we might be able to part with the layers and layers and layers of self-protection. Is it possible we do not need them anymore? Is it possible, even, that all our chasing is the very thing keeping us insulated from Love?

What if I believed to my core that I have nothing to prove?

The Voice keeps on, gently, firmly: *No one is coming to do this for you. No one is coming to rescue you or save you. No one is coming to offer you an answer for you to get behind. This is the work you must do. From the inside out. From the outside in. You must return to me and I will return to you.*

I think a very young version of myself was standing and waiting for someone to swoop in with the answers—a real adult. And that person would know what to do. That person would know the way forward. That person would figure everything out.

And, the still small Voice kept whispering to me: *That person is not coming. That person is you. You, Leeana, get to be brave in your becoming.*

Too many of us are sitting on our hands, looking down at the dirt, waiting for someone to come in and declare our rights to us. What's so sad about this is that we've become increasingly paralyzed, increasingly anxious, increasingly restless, no longer sure if we are someone who has the right or capacity or freedom to begin again.

Isn't it interesting how the Soul Bullies sneak in and pin us down with their thousand tiny threads? We aren't bound and gagged with one giant rope. We are pinned down and paralyzed one untruth at a time. And they add up.

No one is coming to save you. Your mother cannot do this inner work for you. Your partner cannot do this inner work for you. Your church cannot do this inner work for you. And here's the truth: even God cannot do this inner work for you. You must do it. You. This is both the good and bad news. You and I have an opportunity to offer something to ourselves that no one else can offer us. We get to decide if we will pick up the most unwieldy and needy parts of ourselves and bring them to God. Daily. Over and over again. And open ourselves up to his healing work. It is our decision. We decide if we will respond to his invitation or not.

I have wanted to be rescued in my life. I have wanted someone to come in and do the hard work for me. But in those dark early hours of twilight, God comes to me and says, *You and I must do the wrestling if you are to believe that I am Love. No one else. You are the one you have been waiting for.*

I may always walk with a limp as a result of this wrestling; but the limp is my mark of bravery, of engaging instead of escaping.

• • •

Part 2

Brave in the
Becoming

six

Let the Dead Trees Go

Anything or anyone
that does not bring you alive
is too small for you.

David Whyte

I hired some guys to come do a full day of clearing on our property. We have just over an acre of land, most of which is kind of wild and untamed and overgrown. And we like it that way. But every once in a while, it needs to be cut back and cleaned up. We had a few areas in particular that were problematic. Lots of brown palm fronds hanging lifelessly from trees. Two dead trees—one in a prominent location in the front and one in a prominent location in the back. And then there were the weeds, the stumps, and the overgrown grasses that will all become fire hazards as the weather warms up.

I was reluctant to let them cut down the dead trees because . . . well . . . what was it going to look like with them gone?

Makes me think of the ancient story of Gideon, whose name means "he who cuts down." God comes to Gideon while he's hiding, threshing wheat in an underground winepress because the threshing floor was too exposed to the lurking enemy tribe.

God says to Gideon as he is cowering, "Hey there, you mighty warrior. I'm going to use you to save your people from these enemies." And God does. But first, Gideon is instructed to go into his father's camp and cut down the fertility totem and the golden gods and all the props and false promises. He is to get rid of what's not working. Before he went into battle, the dead stuff had to go.

"This entire area is a fire hazard," the guy in the yard told me. He could feel my reluctance. "And this tree right here is actually dead," he said as he pointed to one of the two trees that flanks our gate.

"But if you take this one down, it will be lopsided," I contended. "There'll be a tree on one side and not the other."

"Yeah, but it's *dead*," he reiterated slowly, making eye contact with me.

I acquiesced. It began to feel sort of silly to keep on trying to convince him of the beauty of a carcass.

Gideon was reluctant too. "I'm the runt of the litter," he tells God. "Do not ask me to do this."

"I will go with you," God says. But Gideon wants a sign.

I get it. Bargaining is always part of the grief cycle. *Can't I just hold on to what I have, even if what I have is no longer living?* This all seems very familiar.

As the guys descended with their power equipment, branches began flying furiously. And after a full day's work, things looked different. When you get rid of the brown, the green is much more prominent. When you cut down large dead trees, you can see things that were previously hidden by gray, bony branches. When you pull up stumps and brittle bushes, the landscape you were used to is altered.

It's OK to let the dead trees go. It's OK to pull them up from their roots and carry them off. It's OK to bring in power tools and prune what's brown and withered and no longer thriving.

It's weird at first. I was so used to that big (dead) tree blocking the gazebo. And then it was gone, those grayish fingers that leaflessly reached up to the tiles on the gazebo roof.

I could see things I couldn't see before.

I gritted my teeth and wrote a big check and handed it to the guys and I walked the property and looked at what remained. Now that all the dead was gone. And it was surprising. I thought I would hate how it all looked—naked or bare—but the truth is, it felt like parts of our property could breathe again.

I didn't realize what I couldn't see. I didn't realize what was there until I let the dead trees go.

We let the weeds and the half-dead and the fire hazards hang on. Because we're used to them. Because we don't know what will be left if we hack away what we know. It's scary to acknowledge it, admit it, when something is not working.

Burn it down, I begin to hear in my ear. *Burn it down. Leeana, burn it down.*

"What? What is that supposed to mean?" I ask into the dark. "That's a *Thelma & Louise* phrase, a midlife crisis phrase. Good Christian girls don't 'burn it down.' What are you talking about?"

I needed a sign.

I would be doing my day, going about my life, and I would hear the phrase "Burn it down." So I mentioned to a couple people that this phrase was bouncing around inside me and I didn't totally understand what I was supposed to do with it, and I just kept receiving the encouragement to pay attention. So I did. I paid attention.

And here's what I started noticing: Every time I was distorting myself by propping up an expected façade instead of opening up, *Burn it down* would sound off, like a radar ping growing louder and louder in my gut.

I would be trying to please someone, gain their approval, win them over. And I would hear, *Burn it down.*

I would be trying to overcompensate or keep the peace and keep everyone "happy." And I would hear, *Burn it down.*

I would be trying to appear competent and striving to make a good impression, reaching a bit, pressing a bit. And I would hear, *Burn it down.*

All I can think of is the male peacock. Spreading his big, beautiful feathers to get attention. Knowing just what will attract. Knowing what will be praised. Knowing what will be valued. Knowing what others will find pleasing.

I didn't realize how hard I was trying.

These are the strategies that helped at some point, but now . . . well, now, they are perpetuating unhealth. My need to be thought well of and approved of, my fear of mess, my need to avoid discomfort at all costs—these are not only unhelpful coping mechanisms, they might be toxic. And I just have not had the capacity previously to be as honest as I am now.

I feel that gentle leaning on my soul—revelation, not condemnation—and I know the familiar holy tension. It's something I can explore or ignore. The choice is mine. The free will is mine. And it's OK, either way. I get to choose.

That's the incredible thing about God; he gives us the choice. Some of us have forgotten this. Forgotten our agency, our ability to choose. Perhaps life took a lot of our choices away from us, we fell victim one time too many, and it feels as though our ability to choose was robbed.

But we always have a choice. Always. We always have the choice to say, I'm just not ready. It is a great risk to drop all these protective layers, to burn down what we've relied on. *It is a great risk to trust something Other than our trying.*

I think about Gideon. It was a great risk for him to go into battle. It was a great risk for him to go into his father's camp and burn down all the false hope.

You do not have to be afraid of being yourself anymore.

Burn it down, Leeana. You do not have to be afraid of being yourself anymore.

Whoa.

Sometimes beginning again is about stripping away, burning down, removal. We want to begin again, but something is in the way. I needed to burn down everything standing in the way of my capacity to be honest. Because honesty was the way home. We don't get to the truth while we're deeply invested in what's false.

God asked Gideon to dismantle the darlings, and then he took him into battle after he whittled down Gideon's army to three hundred men. Three hundred men against the enemy's 135,000. The odds were nuts.

For me, the crux of the entire Gideon story is not that he defeated the enemy with an army of three hundred. Or that God spoke to him while he was hiding. Or that God gave Gideon sign upon sign upon meticulously executed sign.

It is that God asks Gideon to go into his own camp and get rid of all the things he and his people had been leaning on and turning to for false security. As long as they were bowing down to hollow hopes, there would never be any victory. But if they could trust something beyond themselves, then there might be some movement.

Burn it down.

All our props.

All our crutches.

All our security systems.

All our vanishing edges.

All our tricks.

All our trying.

All our sleight of hand.

All our false gods.

All the ways, essentially, we're believing we can pull it off without anyone noticing. Except, *we're* noticing. And it's kinda killing us. Because it's dis-integrating us.

I have been meditating on Parker Palmer's concept of living "divided no more" throughout this year. *Burn it down* seemed to always echo in my ear when I was dividing instead of expanding.

Is this thought serving to integrate me or divide me?

Is this behavior serving to integrate me or divide me?

Is this practice serving to integrate me or divide me?

Is this voice serving to integrate me or divide me?

Am I moving in the direction of naked and unashamed or am I moving in the direction of covered and cowering?

Palmer writes that the integrated people "decide no longer to act on the outside in a way that contradicts some truth about themselves that they hold deeply on the inside."[1]

But it's scary—scary to entertain what darlings God might be nudging us to dismantle, which outside actions are betraying or contradicting a deep inner truth that we're afraid to live by. God's call to congruence might require a bit of burning down.

The burning down typically doesn't begin on the outside of us (actions); typically the burning down begins on the inside of us (transformation).

God keeps tapping on my soul and telling me it's time to expand. Expansion isn't notoriety or fame or upward mobility or success. Expansion is ruthlessly confronting what is not working so that what is truly alive can breathe. Expansion is truth-shall-set-me-free honesty. Expansion is wrestling, engaging, listening. It is letting the dead trees go.

God's call to congruence might require a bit of burning down.

Gideon's queasiness and reluctance to God's invitation should bring us some comfort, Barbara Brown Taylor writes, "because they remind us that we do not have to stop being human in order to start being God's."[2] This is a relief. Most of us can't fix ourselves enough to begin again fearlessly. We have to walk on, scared.

I'm sitting at the kitchen table in the earliest twilight, eyes closed. An arm is reaching toward me, gently yet insistent, handing me something. It's a match, like the long matches we used to have in a brass box on our fireplace when I was growing up. Before neon plastic clickers, we had these slender elegant matches that were long enough to light a fire without burning your fingers. Ours sat on the mantel below my grandmother's magnolia painting. My whole life.

Here's a match, Leeana. Would you like to take it?

The morning sky is ablaze today. Pinks, salmons, white-hot orange embers layering upward.

Will I take the match? Will you? Who would we be if we could let go of those ways of being in our lives that are dividing us?

Runt of the Litter becomes Mighty Warrior. Imagine that.

● ● ●

seven

You Weren't Consulted

Forgive yourself for
not knowing
what you didn't know
before you learned it.

Elisha Goldstein

We have six chickens that we let roam around our yard. At first,
when they were young, we'd have to herd them into their coop. But
not long after, as soon as dusk would begin settling in, we couldn't
find the chickens anywhere. We walked around the yard looking
for them, but no chickens.

I walked down to the coop and looked in. No chickens. But
then I heard a rustling, and I put my head all the way into the coop

and looked up, and there in the rafters were six sets of beady eyes staring down at me, all six chickens clutched to a rafter with their prehistoric, fingernailed feet, quivering.

The chickens are programmed with a fear response. They know predators lurk, and so they must find their way to higher ground, to safety, and stay there until it's daylight and safe to come out. But here's the truth: if they stay up there, and listen to fear only, they will starve.

Protection helps us avoid dying, but it doesn't necessarily promote real living.

Protection helps us avoid dying, but it doesn't necessarily promote real living. We developed layers of protection and insulation against the world because that's what it took to grow up in a world that was, at times, hostile to us. We adopted strategies, strengths, subtleties in our personalities in order to maneuver through our lives.

This happened. Unavoidably.

We became larger than we needed to be or smaller than we needed to be. We puffed ourselves up or we shrunk ourselves down. We blended in or we stood on the tallest rock and growled with all our teeth showing. We learned how to change our colors. We figured out how to play dead or squawk aggressively. We got good at waving our feathers, digging a hole, stamping our feet, running for the hills.

These adaptations saved us. We did it. If you're reading this right now, you figured out how to get here. You figured out how to survive the tumult of your life. If you were to stretch your life story out onto a timeline and record the major, formational events in your life, you would see that you have been resilient. You did what you had to do. After all, as I heard someone say recently, "You weren't consulted."

You weren't consulted about your sister's special needs.

You weren't consulted when your parents divorced.

You weren't consulted when the abuse started.

You weren't consulted about your mother's addiction.

You weren't consulted about your father's anger.

You weren't consulted about all the moving.

You weren't consulted when the church split.

You weren't consulted about the mental illness.

You weren't consulted about the financial downturn.

You weren't consulted about the cancer.

You weren't consulted when the mean girls spread lies about you.

You weren't consulted about how you were treated, who listened and who didn't, or what the cost would be.

You weren't consulted.

Nobody took the time, particularly, to ask you if it was all right with you if things blew up.

There you were, needing to survive. And you got incredibly creative. Because that's what we all do. That's what we've all had to do in our own ways. And it's actually a miracle. It's what keeps us on the planet. It's what keeps our species from dying out. It's like a microchip created in us. And it's really, really remarkable.

But (and this is some terrible news I'm about to give you), none of this recuses you.

Because then we become adults who must live in this world with other adults—vulnerably and companionably—and who must

71

also take care of the children in our lives, and the layers that we have packed on so magnificently are now, without much warning, completely in the way of being with these people we love.

Something happened to you, and you weren't consulted. But there will come a day for many of us when our aggressive growls or playing dead or huge feathery displays or chameleonism or hiding will simply no longer work.

Our strategies will cause tension with people we love. Our props will get in the way of intimacy and connection with others and we will feel lonely. Our ways of being will actually keep us from so much of what we want in life—to be known, to be connected, to belong.

Like it or not, the ball is now in our court. We get to choose. "Growth is not an accident. Growth is a process. We have to want to grow. We have to will to move away the stones that entomb us in ourselves."[1]

That line "entomb us in ourselves" is haunting, isn't it? When we refuse to take personal responsibility for what needs to happen going forward, we are participating in the stone-stacking that is entombing us. Now, we are willfully choosing a way that is not life.

We can stare into our phones and put our heads down and anesthetize the wall-hitting, or we can see it for what it is: a door.

God reached out his hand to me and said it was time to go deeper in. Through the fear. Way back when, I wasn't consulted. And I adopted layers of striving and peacekeeping so that I could both stand out and fly under the radar. This worked. Worked well, actually. Until it didn't. And the mustering and hustling and propping began to feel like fertility totems and golden calves instead of freedom.

In order to begin again (every day, every hour, every three minutes) we have to confront our entrenchments, our entombments. We can either actively participate in more stone-stacking or we can actively participate in our own resurrection.

This is not about fixing ourselves. Alchemically, God will use our brokenness. He will come to us when we are hiding and scared. We don't have to be "fixed-up" for God. He will come to us. And if he is coming to you, if he is putting a gentle pressure on your soul, what would it be like to not turn him away? That's all. Just turn toward him and be still and breathe and listen. That's all.

Spoiler alert: you can go ahead and forgive yourself for not figuring all this out earlier. Just plan on it. I derailed myself for some time, angry and self-inflicting, because I didn't somehow see sooner how all these layers of self-protection were actually standing in my way. This is just one more assault of the Soul Bullies, who are using you in your own demise. They don't want you to begin again. They want you stuck. So they will remind you of what a dolt you are that you couldn't find your way within the approved timeline.

Ten, twenty, thirty years ago . . . you weren't consulted. But because of the grace of free will, now you are. Now you get a chance to speak up and to lean in. It's scared-sacred work: after all this time and all these layers and all those strategies, to move away the stones that entomb us in ourselves, to let the too-tight skins be removed, to be awakened, to begin again.

● ● ●

eight

Do Not Feed the Stray Cats

Search me, O God, and know my heart;
Try me and know my anxious thoughts;
And see if there be any hurtful way in me,
And lead me in the everlasting way.

Psalm 139:23–24 NASB

In this scared-sacred work of becoming, the Soul Bullies plant endless false dichotomies, skewing our thinking, so that we stay stuck:

You can either have approval or you can have intimacy.

You can either confront issues and be consumed or you can avoid issues and be paralyzed.

You can either use your voice and make people mad or silence your voice and keep people happy.

Either/or thinking is a red flag, an indication that our thoughts and feelings are under the control of fear and not Love. When I back myself into either/or thinking, it is always a lose-lose: total demise or total denial. Those are my only two choices, neither of which is particularly appealing. When we do this, we start to get very anxious, because our minds and bodies know we have created a too-tight system. No matter which path we take, we can't win, which is a suffocating reality.

But Love offers us a different way of thinking altogether, one that is transcendent and not transactional. Love offers us a third way. *Via media* is Latin for the middle way, the narrow path that cuts between our dichotomies and dualistic thinking. The path to healing and becoming always takes the *via media*, the very narrow way that insists life, real living, is somehow inextricably linked to surrender.

The narrow way requires letting go, burning down, and maybe most of all, trusting in something beyond what we can see.

I was having bouts with an ugly Soul Bully who kept after me, wearing me down. I was especially frustrated with myself that I was still listening to lies, that I couldn't graduate from shame, that I hadn't kicked that voice out for good. I was falling back into a false dichotomy: I must either eradicate shame or be subject to it. The end. But God hinted to me that perhaps it was all a bit more nuanced than that.

I resumed my 5 a.m. waiting for faraway things.

Invite me in, Leeana, the Inner Voice of Love said to me. *Invite me in to the place where you are feeling shaky and self-loathing. Invite me in to the darkest corner of your heart.*

"You're a fool," says this entirely too familiar voice in my head. "Small and shortsighted and unrealistic and unwell and ineffective. You're a fool. You're caught up in your own false fantasy world. You have no voice."

I tell God what the voice is saying to me. I feel embarrassed and exposed. Sometimes we don't jump right to naked and unashamed. We start with naked and ashamed and let God meet us there.

I'm so sorry, Leeana, this is heavy and attacking and vicious. Do you believe this voice? Do you believe it knows you?

"Yes," I say without hesitation, "I believe it knows me better than anyone. It knows I'm cheating my way through life, fooling everyone."

My entire body feels like lead, but I have to tell the truth.

This voice, Leeana, is not serving you. In your head, you know that voice is trouble. But in your body, it reigns. You are serving the Soul Bullies and they are no longer serving you. I need you fleshier, more exposed, more vulnerable.

"How do I stop serving their shame? Why do I believe their voices?"

They have been the loudest, most convincing voices. Others have joined in, corroborating their story. People you have needed to offer a different narrative have not been able to. You have been drawn to and trusted people who told you the same story because that is the familiar story. Leeana, there's a new narrative in town.

Can you hang in there when things are not going well and not turn to that vicious voice for comfort?

"Why does it bring me comfort?"

It's easier to believe than to trust you are truly free. Freedom scares you. It's both what you want so deeply and also what scares you the very most. **You run back to that vicious voice because it keeps you in your place, and that is comforting to you.**

You believe this voice knows you best, sees who you really are. But what if it doesn't? You are terrified of your greatness. You are terrified of yourself. You are terrified of not having that net to fall back into. The net that keeps you small and self-loathing and Victim. What will you have then? Who will you be? Who will you become?

What if you broke off your relationship with, addiction to, that voice?

What would we have if we didn't have our distorted narratives to nurture? What would we have if we didn't have our disordered attachments to protect? They have become a living, breathing entity in our lives, a prominent character in the story line.

What are you asking to keep you safe that has no investment in your safety whatsoever? What are you turning to for security and comfort that does not actually care about your security and comfort? What are you asking to save you that will never save you, has no interest in saving you, and in fact, has no capacity to save you?

That toxic voice is like a golden calf to me. I bow down to it, listen to it, trust it, even though it's completely hollow.

Change, Fr. Richard Rohr says, is typically when something new begins. But the mystery of transformation is something different. Transformation is not when something new begins but when something old falls apart. And this disorientation of things falling apart is what nudges us into new ways of thinking. Otherwise, perhaps we would never go on our own volition.

Everything in us resists the old falling apart.

> The pain of something old falling apart—chaos—invites the soul to listen at a deeper level. It invites and sometimes forces the soul to go to a new place because the old place is falling apart. Otherwise most of us would never go to a new place. . . . You will do anything to keep the old thing from falling apart.[1]

The problem with allowing the old to fall apart is that we are afraid of what it's going to cost us. And like many of you, I don't know if I have it in me to pay.

The cost, to me, would be a more complete surrender than I had previously experienced, which means a deeper trust than I have ever allowed myself to practice. And what I can tell you now, at the risk of getting ahead of myself, is that the anticipation of all this was much more difficult than the actual passage through. The passage through ended up being a relief. The anticipation of pain, the fear of being in pain, was the hardest part.

We see that our way of doing or being is no longer working, and so we are confronted with either nurturing it, gripping it, holding tightly to it, attaching ourselves even more deeply to it, or unhanding it.

Maybe the things you are serving feel as though they *are* still serving you. This is fine. You are where you are, and you cannot be where you are not. And you are not yet ready.

Someday, though, you may be walking down the street, innocuously, and you will all of a sudden have an epiphany. You will realize that these things actually aren't serving you in any way:

Your keeping the peace at all costs, even in a toxic situation

Your crowd-building

Your need to keep everyone happy

Your clinging to certainty

Your harbored resentment

Your need to appear competent

Your belief in the voices of self-loathing and self-bullying

You will be watching a kids' soccer game in the rain or you will be picking out artichokes at Trader Joe's or you will be inside the whoosh of the car wash or you will be sitting at your desk working on spreadsheets or you will be staring out a window. In other words, you will likely be somewhere unspectacular or unassuming

And *shizam!*, the faraway thing you have been waiting for will arrive—maybe because you created a soft place for it to land—and you will know something you did not know the minute previously. You will know that you are deeply entrenched in a relationship with some behavior or substance or person or past, and you have been giving it your all, and it is giving you nothing but trouble in return.

And you will be ready.

I didn't anticipate needing to confront companions on my journey. I just assumed I wanted to be rid of them but in reality somehow felt a familiar fondness for them, and therefore was more reluctant than I realized to part company.

God asked me a question I was not ready for. He said, *What if shame isn't your greatest enemy after all? What if shame is actually your dearest friend? What if you are more attached to this shame-stance*

79

than you realize? What if your greatest fear is being rid of it? What would you have then, if you didn't have this self-condemnation?

That vicious voice is comforting in a weird way. It is the voice I recognize more than any other. What would I be left with if it was no longer with me?

You are allowed to leave it, Leeana. Unhook from it. Not need it anymore. You are allowed to believe something else. You are allowed to be comfortable with your own strength.

I want so deeply to be out of my spirals, free from the closed loops in my own mind. But I hadn't expected what I heard. I hadn't even considered that I was nourishing shame, protecting it, that it was a closer companion than I care to admit. So close, in fact, I recognize its voice more clearly than my own voice, than the voice of God. This is the honest truth. I hear the voice of shame and it is the most familiar thing to me. Its viciousness is so familiar to me, I have to consciously dissent.

What's scary is that I want to be rid of it, and yet, I keep going back to it. I keep giving it power. I keep sliding into its narrative.

For some of us, it's fear. Or anger. Resentment. Regret. Contempt. Control. Our victim status. **We want to be free, but we also don't.** Because we believe these companions have served us, or at least they have kept us from being alone. What would we have if we no longer had fear? What would we be left holding? What would we have if we no longer had anger? What would we have to face if we no longer harbored contempt? What would we talk about if we no longer talked about "them" or "those people" or "that community" like we've become so accustomed to doing?

Starving shame is hard. All I want to do is feed it. Buy into its story. Over and over again. I believe, like with the stray cat, if I feed it, it will go away. But what happens? It now knows where its nourishment is coming from and so it stays on. Happily. Crying for more food. Warm milk. Pawing at the door. Back for more. Let me in. Let me in. Let me in. Let me curl up on your couch and warm your feet forever.

This is not the work we are doing. We are not feeding the stray cats. Because it is never enough. They are never appeased. They are never filled.

These disordered attachments are engines too. They motivate us in some strange way. They give us energy for productivity and performance. They drive us to achieve. In other words, there is often a payoff for staying in an intimate relationship with a disordered attachment.

But what good is it to gain everything . . . but ultimately lose?

Once this disordered attachment has been brought to our attention, we now know something significant. We can't, now, unknow what has been revealed.

Once you begin to confront your own attachments, securities, pet pathologies, and once you sense God inviting you to hand them to him, you will know something transformative is happening. *But transformation always requires us to leave something behind.* And that's never easy.

This has nothing to do with behaving better, cleaning up our act. This is simply about granting God access to each layer, one by one, as we are able. This is opening up instead of covering up. Honesty before God.

God has come to me in the dark of morning and suggested my attachment. He's named something for me—that I am closer to shame than I wanted to admit—and as I drink down my coffee and stare out the window beyond the hills as the rose gold is starting to streak the sky, I know what I didn't know the minute previously.

I know that God is offering me a *via media*, a third way, as he always does. My journey isn't about either eradicating shame or being subject to it. My journey, for the foreseeable future, is going to be the daily, hourly, minute-to-minute surrender of shame. Admitting, over and over again, my tendency to want to nourish those stray cats and, instead, allowing God to speak over me.

• • •

nine

Surrounded by a Great Cloud of Witnesses in Target

You are the place where I stand
on the day when my feet are sore.

Wes Carry

As any mother knows, when your husband is traveling, and all your planning and creative strategies and Amazon Prime-ing have fallen through, you have to do the thing you are always trying to avoid at all costs: you have to take all your kids to Target with you.

That's OK. We're just going to zip in and zip out and be home before anyone even realizes it. I just need paper plates and dry shampoo (obviously).

Unfortunately, I had made the fatal error of getting my kids a Slurpee after school as a way to woo (bribe) them into good behavior. In retrospect this was a terribly flawed plan, because I basically gave them speedballs and then begged them to sit still.

I'm in the paper goods section, and I see that my Luke and Lane have pulled out all the oversized blocks of bulk toilet paper from the shelf, have stuffed Elle onto the shelf, and are now walling her in while she screams in horror and delight. Brick by brick. Buried alive by Charmin. It is Poe's *Cask of Amontillado* right there in the toilet paper aisle of Target.

A woman is standing by herself in this very same section and she is clearly horrified by my children. Not even horrified. Angry.

Let me pause and say that they were behaving like animals, like an episode of the Herdman kids, but still, I was totally unprepared for what happened next.

She begins talking about how horribly behaved my kids are, how she would have never let her kids act this way in public, how awful the parenting is these days, and how these kids are going to hurt someone. She is not actually looking at me. She is saying all this while still looking at the Ziploc bags.

She keeps going, looking straight ahead and saying, "These kids are *awful*. They practically ran me over."

She is not speaking directly to me. She will not look at me. But she is clearly talking to me, and what she was saying was so vitriolic, so hateful, that I froze. I cannot think of one thing to say to her. I cannot believe what is happening. I can only gather my kids awkwardly and get away.

As we walk away, I get teary as Lane asks, "Mom, what was that woman saying?" and I feel all my depletion rush into the moment. All of a sudden I can't remember the last time I took a shower. I can't remember if I even brushed my teeth that day. I can't remember if I am wearing a bra or underwear or if I should even be out of the house. I can't remember what time of day it is or what I had come to the store to get.

"She was being unkind," I say. "And . . . you guys can't destroy Target."

I begin thinking of all the things I could have said to her, and even consider marching back over to her with some select words.

I wish I would have told her that my husband was gone on a trip and I had been parenting alone for longer than I cared to count. I wish I would have asked her if she'd like to help instead of insult me. I wish I would have told her that I thought her shoes were horrible.

But I keep pushing my cart of paper plates toward the checkout, with my slightly broken heart and three sugared kids running circles around me. I feel small and "in trouble" and young. And I completely abandon my adult resources. I stand there, in elementary school, self-conscious and committed to anything that will keep me from feeling embarrassed.

My phone rings.

"Hi, T," I say. It's Tina calling.

"Hey, Lee, are you in Target? Laurel said she just saw you and the kids in another aisle."

"Yes, I am in Target. I'm near the checkout."

As I'm saying those words, Tina and her young daughter, Laurel, come into view, smiling, arms out.

"Are you OK?" she says right as she sees me, the look on my face clearly telling the whole story.

I tell her all about how a lady with horrible shoes just tore me a new one in the toilet paper aisle.

And Tina immediately walks with me to the registers and helps herd the crew as waves of anxiety are still shocking through my body.

"Oh, Lee," she says. "I want to go back and trip her."

She gets me safely in line and then goes to look at some flowers behind me.

"Leedles," I hear one of my many nicknames called out in front of me.

I look up and there is Linsey. Alone.

"Are you OK?" she says, my face still obviously drained.

Tina rejoins me and tells Linsey the entire story. Of the lady. And the kids. While Linsey shakes her head and looks me right in the eye. Tina passes me and my crew off to Linsey.

Linsey takes my keys and two of my kids by the hand and stays with me all the way to my car. She helps my kids get buckled in and she hugs me. Linsey doesn't even like to hug. She says in my ear, "You're doing it."

Tina has known me since I was eleven. Linsey has known me since I was eighteen. Two of my very best friends in the entire world just happened to be at the Rancho San Diego Target on a day when I was getting shredded by a stranger.

It's practically intolerable to be so deeply disapproved of and to have to tell people about it, all while being seen with greasy hair and lunatic children while, possibly, wearing no bra. I can't say for sure.

It's practically intolerable to see the looks of concern and compassion on Tina's and Linsey's faces. I'd rather them not see me like this. Even two of my dearest friends. I'd rather them see me in control, "strong," perfect. In my current state, the Soul Bullies are telling me that I didn't just receive a stranger's disapproval, I am now at risk of receiving my friends' disapproval.

But I tolerate it. I have to. Love is taking my car keys and holding Elle's hand. Love is putting my items in my car and chatting with my kids. Love is handing me my purse. Love is asking me, "Is there anything else you need?" Love texts me later to check in.

I get to stand still in the middle of my life instead of run circles around it. I get to practice being painstakingly open instead of slamming shut. I get to be held. Lucky me. It wears the toxic shame right out of me.

St. John of the Cross wrote,

"What is grace," I asked God.
And He said,
"All that happens."

I have a hunch this might be true. I have a hunch that every wall could be a door. Even a toilet paper wall in Target reinforced by a woman's awful words could become a door that leads to Love.

● ● ●

87

ten

Bullying vs. Believing

It's as if there is a part of you that so rails against being
shattered by love that you shatter yourself first.

Geneen Roth

I went to see Beth, my spiritual director, as I do every month because she is someone who can help me find meaning when all I
see is desolation.

We do not do this soul work in isolation. Period. This deep work
requires the presence of an empathetic other. You don't need a
crowd. You need a trained person, who can listen without fixing,
who is committed to you, who can point you back to God's voice
in your life. Someone who won't subtly sabotage you because of
his or her own stuff. Someone who won't decide you're getting a
little too liberated and will try to sneakily cut you off at the knees
with contempt or whining. Someone who has the capacity to hold

space for whatever it is you're working through without getting triggered and crazy and handsy with your life.

Beth is one of these empathetic others. I've been seeing her since we returned home from the Middle East five years ago. Back then we sat on her patio—a suspended patio attached to what felt like a tree house perched above a canyon of eucalyptus. She held space for my anxiety and exhaustion, she poked holes in the lies, she ushered me into the presence of God through prayer, she helped tie me to Truth. She encouraged me, back then too, to open all the portals of my life—wide open—and let Love in.

Beth is a surfer and a mystic and she wears her hair in locks with a portion pulled back from her face. Five years ago was actually not the first time I met Beth. I saw her one time, fifteen years ago, when Steve and I were engaged and I was living in San Diego and he was living on the other side of the world. The war was raging, and soon he would take leave and come home and we would get married and then head back to the other side of the world together for our first year of marriage. This was both exhilarating and insane. And something inside my body, which was buzzing and hopped-up, knew all this.

I was given Beth's number by a dear friend who told me to just go and talk with her. So I met with her in a candlelit room on floor cushions with a cross nearby and she witnessed a fury of feelings and fears. I don't consider it a coincidence that Beth and I found each other again, ten years later. So I've stuck close to her.

I told her about walking through the house and opening everything up. I told her that I no longer wanted to be invested in keeping things shut. I wanted to be honest, to confront anything creating division or falseness inside of me, to stop being afraid.

I'm telling Beth all this, when she declares a proclamation that makes me almost spit out my coffee:

"Well, Leeana, I think we should henceforth refer to this summer as 'the summer of making love to yourself.'"

Good grief, Beth.

She's dead serious. "This is the time to listen to and care for yourself like you never have before."

But of course she went on: "This summer is about taking the most tender care of yourself. It's about learning what you need and what you are craving and hungry for. It's about holding yourself and listening to yourself and responding to yourself in the most loving way possible."

This is getting awkward.

I write Beth a check and hug her and thank her and walk to my car slightly hazy about what it means, exactly, to kick off the summer of making love to myself. So I tried to think about the whole concept in terms of someone else.

If a dear friend called me—someone I truly love—and she told me she was feeling stuck and scared and tired, I'd say, "Come over immediately."

When she walked in the door, I would be sure she had all the beverages. Hydration and caffeination. I would know how she likes her coffee and I'd have it waiting for her. I'd know if she likes ice water, water with no ice, or sparkling water. And I'd have it waiting for her. I'd take out (and actually light) the expensive Anthropologie candle and I'd pet her arm.

I wouldn't say, "Gah, do you know how many times you've needed prayer this month? You are such a mess. I can't *take* it any more." No, I'd meet her in the middle. I'd sit with her. I'd love her. I'd listen. I'd suspend judgment or clever advice. I'd be a witness to her struggle so she would know she isn't alone.

But how often do I sit with myself in this way? How often do I maintain this posture with myself? Don't I always assume that bullying, prodding, and degrading is the way into change, when it comes to me? If I can just be hard enough on myself, I will get it this time.

Sometimes I sit down and make two lists:

1. How do I think about, talk about, and talk to my dear friends?
2. How do I think about, talk about, and talk to myself?

It's actually a very telling exercise.

For far too many of us, though certainly not all of us, our first instinct is to starve, push, condemn, convict, beat up, criticize, scold, demean, lecture ourselves into new territory. *If I can just convince myself of how bad I am, then I will make changes.*

This is slavery. And it will not last.

We do not punish ourselves into transformation. We do not begin again by refusing to forgive ourselves. I've come to believe that we make lasting changes because we know, somewhere inside us, that we deserve something better, that we were hardwired for wholeness.

I just read recently that the etymology of the word *forgiveness* is "to give up the desire or power to punish."[1] Man. Giving up the desire or power to punish ourselves is taking ourselves down from the giant hook of regret.

91

Forgiving ourselves for covering up, holding up, propping up
. . . when what was needed was opening up. We didn't know. Or,
if we did, we just weren't ready. Can we forgive ourselves for being
where we *are* and not where we wish we had been? Can we see
that we are inching toward where we always hoped we could be?

I sat with Beth through the summer, over and over again. I felt

**Can we forgive
ourselves for being
where we *are* and
not where we wish
we had been?**

stupid for not seeing how invested I always am
in protecting myself. I felt stupid and angry
at myself for contributing to unhelpful and
unhealthy dynamics in my home. I felt im-
mature and avoidant for not being willing to
be more honest. I felt frustrated that I didn't
deal with this all sooner.

And Beth said to me over and over again that I would, when I
felt ready, look at my regret eye to eye, and forgive myself for what
I did or didn't do.

We don't make lasting, constructive changes in our lives because of shame or self-loathing. We finally decide we were made
for something more. This might come to us as a very small sense
of knowing, but it's a change in perspective, and it is the soil for
new life.

The first time I realized I was experiencing acute anxiety, I
couldn't catch my breath. My chest was burning and my pulse
was racing, and I was helpless. My body felt like a runaway train.
I was sitting at my desk writing, in my bedroom, and the physical
sensation of anxiety escalated so intensely and so quickly that I
got up and walked straight into my bathroom and got directly in
the shower because I didn't know what else to do to calm myself

down. I couldn't think. I couldn't breathe. My heart pounded. My throat felt tight.

I stood in the shower for a very long time. And finally, after the water and the steam and the white noise had had their time to work on me, my body began to unknot. My throat and chest opened incrementally. My breath returned.

I walked out of the shower and into my robe. I didn't dry off or brush out my hair, which was a nest now. And I walked from the bathroom straight to my bed and I went to sleep.

My college roommate used to always say, "I know when you're stressed because I walk into our dorm room in the middle of the day, and you're asleep." She was so right. My immediate reaction to anxiety is to want to turn it off, and the only way I can do that is to sleep.

I love sleep. I crave it. It is true rest for me when the waking hours are fitful. And that day, working at my desk until I couldn't anymore, until my body reached such a fever pitch that I couldn't think, I wondered for the first time, *Hey, maybe this isn't normal.*

The peak of anxiety leads to the valley of depression, and this is—as so very many of you well know—a cycle that takes most of our energy to manage. We make contact with life, but we cannot connect to it. People, beauty, rich experiences bounce off us. And it's not OK.

I have hushed conversations in the bleachers at baseball games and in the corner of a friend's kitchen about all this. It's an epidemic, really. All these vibrant and brilliant and creative and hilarious and nurturing men and women who are suffering behind closed doors. Riding tidal waves within their bodies.

If you struggle with any mental health challenges, then you know all too well how tending is one of the first things out the window when we are feeling anxious or depressed or both. You cannot maintain a routine. Beginning again and again with the small beats of life just isn't possible, or so it feels.

Chopping veggies, washing skin, brushing hair, drinking water, walking roads, seeing bougainvillea, hearing laughter, reading poems, changing clothes. We find that we can pull off the big things in life, but investing ourselves, again and again, in the tending of the little things seems absolutely undoable.

In addition to self-forgiveness, I decided the "summer of making love to myself" would also be about nurturing my capacity for tending. That meant medication, sleep, drinking water, eating vegetables, lots of breathing, and talking to myself as I would a friend instead of an enemy. Being on my own team.

Wherever we're trying to go, we do not bully ourselves there. We believe ourselves there.

Wherever we're trying to go, we do not bully ourselves there. We believe ourselves there.

The soul has a voice. It will tell us what it needs. By soul, here, I mean that part of us that is, itself, transcendent and so always seeking to align with transcendent time, transcendent meaning, transcendent love. It's the part of us that is playing by different rules. Not the keeping-score, keeping-track, keeping-up rules. Instead, the rules of investigation and curiosity and, especially, joining. I've started thinking about the Spirit as something that is flowing, and our souls are always pointing us to that flow, wanting to join it. Our souls are telling us how to heal.

And so, I tie my turquoise tennies while the kids are at gymnastics camp. I walk out of my house, down my driveway, down the long stretch of our single-lane street, then around the corner and up the hill. It is not yet hot-hot. The road dips and rises. Air moves across my face. I keep going, aware that this walking is an act of self-forgiveness, an act of tending, with exceptional care, to my body.

The early months of this year, into spring, have been unusually rainy, and so our neighborhood is overgrown and lush. By this time of year, so much is typically crispy and browned. But not this year. Everything has grown.

I walk down a long stretch of straight road, past a blue house I love, and I stop at a wooden fence with my-very-favorite bougainvillea pouring over it, littering the pavement with pink. In the hulking overgrowth are shades of salmon, fuchsia. Piped into my ears are the voice and words of the poet Naomi Shihab Nye and her well-worn lines: "Before you know what kindness really is you must lose things," and I know she's right.

● ● ●

Part 3

Holy
Awakening

eleven

A Threshold

The horizon leans forward,
Offering you space to place new steps
of change.

Maya Angelou

When I was a sophomore in college, I finally made a decision about a boy I had been seeing back home. We had been very close in high school and our relationship was carrying over to college, but now we were long-distance and we were, looking back, trying to find a way to say goodbye to each other. The goodbye was the long, slow ripping of a Band-Aid.

And once it was finished, really finished, I did the thing most women do in this situation: I cut off my hair.

I went to the salon and told the girl to cut it. I saw ten inches of my thick blonde waves falling to the floor and I felt some sort of truth entering into my bones. Somehow, ridding myself of that hair was different than, say, changing the color. There was something incredibly important about letting go as a symbol of what had just occurred in my life relationally.

I walked out of the salon feeling emboldened, because I had finally let go of something I had been clinging to. And I'm not talking about my hair, here.

The first time I washed it after the cut, I couldn't believe how good it felt to have so little hair and to feel the water straight onto my neck in the shower. What took years, literally years, to become clear . . . all of a sudden was clear. And I chopped my hair as a symbol of finally knowing.

We do all sorts of things to commemorate awakenings in our lives—get tattoos, cut our hair, paint the house, purge all our clutter. Awakenings are sacred. Crossing thresholds in our lives is sacred. New territory. Knowing we will not go back.

As we are participating in the work of letting the dead trees go, of our own integration, the door has now opened to us. But here we are, distinctly facing the threshold. The threshold, if crossed, represents a point of no return, a point of knowing that cannot be erased.

You will sense a threshold, a point at which you can either pass through or turn around. Regardless of what you choose, it's OK. You are still loved. You are still worthy. You are still held by God.

But if you do decide to cross the threshold, you will become more awake. This is good and scary, and you likely will not be able to go back, you will not let yourself go back. Because once you wake up and see that you were, in fact, slightly dozed off, you will want to protect your awareness.

This kind of beginning again requires us to pay attention.

You will look back and wonder how you got to this point. The path will be a veritable scribble-scrabble. But here you are, nonetheless. You will see so much winding that the path itself won't look like any path at all. But then, just maybe, you will make out a winding that coils in and in and in, and you will see that each lap around has brought you closer to the threshold you now stand before. The gap has closed, incrementally, with each pass.

The word *threshold* has convoluted origins. It quite literally means "point of entering," but the etymology suggests that a threshold may have been "a threshing area adjacent to a living area of a house."[1] A place where the work was done, where the wheat was separated from the chaff.

Chaff is the inedible, scaly skin that surrounds the edible goodness of the crop. Threshing removes this skin. So the threshing area was the place where the work of separation was done. The work of shedding. Like Eustace, undragoned, as Aslan removed one self-protecting dragon skin after the other until Eustace was transformed back into a boy.[2] Crossing the threshold is often about shedding, not adding.

Last spring, I knew that an invitation from God was on the horizon, and I knew I wanted to respond wholeheartedly to that invitation. And I also wished I could just go on vacation from having to be an alive and awake person in the world.

I had spent an entire season searching for my voice, meeting up with my desires, refusing to apologize for myself, taking up my God-appointed space in this world. These were new-ish practices for me, intentionally stirring-from-sleep the me that had always been there but was hiding.

101

When you do this work, when you decide to do this sacred work, you will come to a point at which you are at an impasse. You will be ready to grow, super-duper gung ho about becoming the more brazen you. And then you will begin to realize that you have ways of being and ways of relating that will not allow for this becoming. You will be so ready until you see what must be lost in order for you to be found.

And it's a bit of a shocker, can I just say.

It will start deep down, a low knowing. You will know what needs to change. Your wise old woman within will join hands with God and they will begin to collude. They will lean on your soul, applying a gentle pressure. They will create just enough tension to get your attention. And so, right there, you will be given an invitation, a choice.

They will tell you it is time, but only if you want it to be. They will not coerce you into anything. They'll just show you that a door has presented itself and you are now aware of it. You must choose to walk through, walk across the threshold of shedding and separating, or freeze, or walk away.

Whatever you choose, they will be with you.

You will not be left or abandoned. God will not be disgusted with you. Ever. In that way, God is not like the people in your life. God doesn't tire of your struggle and your back-and-forth and your uncertainty. God doesn't grow weary of your winding path.

The walking-through or walking-away decision will likely come again. I think God is continually inviting us into this work—because he is good and because he loves us—but he lets us decide if we are ready. And it's OK if we're not. It's OK if we're not ready. When we are ready, we will still be scared and reluctant and queasy, but we will *know*. We will know deep down that it is time, that we are willing, and that in order for the new thing to be born, an old thing will need to die.

Certain days, even the love of God will not feel nearly enough. You will feel more like you are hanging on a limb than walking a path, and no one's companionship or counsel will matter at that particular moment. You will feel totally alone, even though you are not.

The aloneness may make you freeze for a time. But if it's truly your time to cross the threshold, you will begin again and you will somehow be given the resources — if you are willing — to take each next step.

God doesn't grow weary of your winding path.

You might even be so lucky as to receive a kind of proof you are on the right track, maybe a sign of some sort. This is such a significant grace   a pocket of provision that will sustain you and maybe even urge you on just the tiniest bit.

Watch for these signs, these microscopic wonders that will support your *knowing*. Space in your chest, a bit more breath in your lungs, a sense of having your feet firmly on the ground and the slightest bit more ease in your own skin. Tears, too.

Everything you hear may be saying the same thing. Every word, concept, idea is actually all the same message when it lands. This is a sign. When everywhere you go you are hearing the same song, that is God talking.

Obviously there will be a hurricane of tension and misgivings. What would life be without the most impossible contradictions swirling through our bodies and souls? But there might also be this sense of invitation that is both winsome and compelling, and it will pull at your soul. Because the soul loves to be invited toward goodness and wholeness.

Once you are on the other side of the door, you tend to not go back. For better or worse. Some of the people in your life would wish you were back on the other side, where you were sleep-living and less particular.

You might look back and see that all along God had offered you doors. You might look back and see there were times and opportunities to walk across the threshold and for any number of reasons you didn't have the resources or the courage or the desire or the energy or the trust. You couldn't be sure that what was waiting for you on the other side of the door was worth it. You believed it would cost too much, and so you didn't pass through. And it's OK.

I thought that the greatest cost I could pay would be letting go of my strategies and my false hopes and facing the truth. And so I worked hard at looking away and explaining away and running away. I know now that the greatest cost I can pay is the debt of dishonesty—with God and with myself. The truth is the only thing that can set us all free.

We will stand still. We will turn and face the very thing we do not want to face, and we will see—eye to eye—what we didn't want to look at all along. We will be scared-sacred. We will be invited. Gently, compassionately, lovingly invited. We must be brave.

Earlier this year I saw a performance by the San Diego Dance Theater. The name of the production was "Janus: And Other Dances of Beginnings, Transitions, and Endings." The opening remarks described the mythological Roman god Janus, who was the god of beginnings, gates, transitions, time, doorways, passages, endings. Having two faces, he looks both backward to the past and forward to the future.

The cover of the playbill showed the silhouettes of two women, back to back, looking in opposite directions. These two women would be the dancers in the first dance, a movement that depicted past and future making peace with each other.

Here's what that looked like for me . . .

• • •

twelve

Bring Her to Me

What has remained separated and unreachable will let itself
be drawn into the love you have been able to receive. One day
you will discover that your anguish is gone. It will leave you
because your weakest self let itself be embraced by your love.

Henri Nouwen

Inside me, there is a nine-year-old me who is looking at life like a
deer in the headlights. She's made entirely of a thousand raw nerve
endings. She's both frozen and skittish, and she's deeply needy.
She wants my time and my attention and my constant care. And
she *deserves* all the love in the entire world. She *deserves* time and
attention and constant care.

But there's just one problem: *I cannot give her everything she
needs.*

Each day, I load her onto my back and I carry her around with me, tending to her neediness and her shame, trying to help her feel better, trying to convince her she's worthy. She is so fragile and vulnerable that I could never leave her alone. I could never abandon her. She requires total attention. I let her lead me out into the world, looking for evidence that she is OK. I give her power.

But then Elle goes through two weeks of preschool boycotting, and I must parent Elle, as a grown-up, from a place that is deeper than fear and the worry that I will mess everything up. I must be the adult, walking Elle through her tears and concerns, and I can barely do it because that nine-year-old is howling inside.

I come back to the darkness of another dawn, exhausted because I am panicked about the situation with Elle. If I leave her at school crying, I will abandon her, which is not an option. If I bring her home, withdraw her from preschool, I feel reactionary, like I am making a decision just to get the discomfort to go away for both of us. I'm caught, and you know how much I hate that feeling.

I begin telling God how I'm feeling—caught, frozen, terrified, paralyzed, desperately afraid that Elle will feel abandoned by me. And in the thin space of that morning, as I am writing furiously, I begin to realize I am no longer writing about Elle. I am writing about me.

I cannot off-load this precious me I am carrying around. Not even for a second. She needs my constant vigilance and watchful eye. She cannot withstand abandonment. But her need is swallowing me whole.

God whispers to me as gently as possible in that early morning: *You are allowed to care for her and move beyond her. You are not leaving her. You are not abandoning her. You are honoring her.*

You are rescuing her. You believe that if you grow beyond her, she will be forgotten, that her story will be forgotten. She needs love and attention, yes, but she is not where you end.

I will take care of her. You do not have to carry her. Bring her to me. I will take care of her so you can walk into the world freely and with open arms.

Come to me and I will give you rest.

Bring her to me. She is precious and wounded and wide-eyed and wild-eyed and I will care for her so that you can keep going. Go, Leeana. Go. Be free.

She is so fragile, practically injured. Keeping up with her and taking care of her is exhausting me.

Yes, bring her to me and I will meet her needs. Nothing you can do will heal her except bringing her to me. Her healing will also heal you.

You are afraid to betray her. You are the only one who can bring her to me. No one else has that right or ability. I cannot even come and take her from you. You must bring her to me. Surrender her. You must choose if you're ready. There is a part of you that feels most safe when you are with her, nursing her wounds. You have purpose and distraction. But it's keeping you from other things, now. You have tended to her. You have loved her. You have watched her, vigilantly. Now it's my turn. Bring her to me so I can send you out.

You can give yourself a gift that no one else can give you. In return, I will give you a gift too. Freedom.

Are you ready?

I am disrupted. A disruption is a breaking apart. And that is God's exact invitation to me, to break apart from my over-responsibility of her and to leave her with Someone who can watch her and feed her and care for her while I go out into the world. This is, ironically, exactly what the preschool teacher is saying to me about Elle: "I will take care of her. Now it is time for you to go. Leave Elle with me." No wonder this has triggered me so deeply. No wonder.

I am receiving permission to form a different kind of relationship with my young self, but it all begins with taking her down off my back, to stop hoisting her up and lugging her around. God tells me I can always come back and visit her, check on her, rub her arm, make sure she's doing OK. But I cannot load her on my back anymore. Trying to fix her is not ever going to be my job. And each time I try, I must bring her to him again. And then do it again. And again. Each day. Each hour. Until I don't have to anymore. Maybe every day for the rest of my life I will be tempted to pick her up and to hold her, but this is not what I am to do, because ultimately she drains my every resource. I honor her and myself best by getting her the care she needs.

A part of me feels safest as her caretaker. My role is clear, my duties defined. I am to keep her as comfortable as possible, no matter the cost. And if I don't, she will wail until I put her on my back again.

It's an enmeshed relationship, to be sure. I am exhausted by her and I'm addicted to her. I want to be rid of her, want to reject her insane neediness and swirling shame and self-consciousness, and I also have no idea what I would do with myself if I surrendered her.

But here is what I know for sure: if I do not hand her over to God, I will forever be codependent on her needs, and I will never be able to be a whole person—for myself or for anyone else.

So I do it. In the early morning hours, I unload her from my back and I look at her, wild-eyed, and I hand her to God. "I love you," I tell her, "and if I continue to look at my life through your eyes, I will serve your fear and your desperate desire for approval. And these are no longer serving me. So I'm going to give you to Someone who can take care of you way better than I ever could."

It was a case of Christ's strength moving in on my weakness. . . . And so the weaker I get, the stronger I become.[1]

God invited me to take her off my back and put her down in front of me where I had to look at her. Really look at her. Which I did not want to do. FOR THE LIFE OF ME. This meant detaching from her enough to actually look at her because that is what she needed most, why she was globbed on to my back in the first place. She needed to be seen, listened to, honored, not just hoisted up and carried. But if you're like me, you will do anything to avoid having to look at this deeply frozen part of yourself. It's so scary.

Then God invites me, in the dark of one random Monday morning to pick up my fragile nine-year-old self and bring her to him. Put her in his arms. Let him care for her. I am terrified, of course, because I do not want to leave her. I do not want to abandon her. And he says, "Bring her to me."

I do, because I want to learn how to love someone or something without losing myself in their power.

• • •

thirteen

Love Is the Fuel

There is no fear in love. But perfect love drives out
fear, because fear has to do with punishment. The
one who fears is not made perfect in love.

1 John 4:18 NIV

So many mornings I would have my time at the kitchen table and
then as the sun was coming up I would be drawn to walk outside
and watch as the sky changed. I'd be barefoot, still in my pajamas,
with a blanket over my shoulders, hunched over my coffee. And
I'd stare for just a few minutes. Breathing. They say it takes fifteen
seconds of looking to lock in the beauty.

The morning of the "bring her to me" conversation with God,
I took a steaming hot shower right after that conversation, as I
knew it would help my body seal in the work of the dialogue. I

had been waiting for over a decade to understand the weight I was carrying around, and when God showed me, he told me to seal it in.

I dropped my head and let hot water percuss my shoulders for some time. I focused on deep breaths. That was it. Nothing magical. Just a small ritual to help my body remember.

I had secretly thought, in a place that I could not unlock, the best I could hope for in life was approval. I'd be lucky to get approval, and if I were to garner it, this sanction, this permission, this endorsement from the world would be enough. Maybe it wasn't as good as the stuff other people got. Love, for example. But, hey, if you can't have love, approval ain't bad. Right?

Eugene Peterson writes about the ecstasy of crowds, how crowds can be a way we attempt to transcend our humanity. Like drug and alcohol abuse and illicit sex, crowds are a way we try to make ourselves feel better about ourselves. Not just the ecstasy of an in-person crowd, but also the ecstasy of an online crowd. Crowds feel good. Crowds clap and yell their approval.

But approval isn't love.

Contact isn't connection.

Image isn't intimacy.

None of this approval-seeking is the real problem, though. *The down-deep problem is that somewhere along the way we began believing the idea that we were never going to get love.*

I am just now quiet enough, still enough, to hear this.

When I opened the door to "burn it down" and welcomed it in, I told Linsey. I told her something new had arrived and I didn't know why it had come or what I was supposed to do with it.

Later, she texted me the following passage, saying it had come to mind soon after I shared "burn it down" with her.

> When you walk through the fire of oppression,
>   you will not be burned up;
>   the flames will not consume you.[1]

We assume that if we burn down the props and safety nets and protections, then *we* will be consumed as well. We will be annihilated in the fire along with our coping mechanisms and strategies and attachments. If we remove the stilts we're standing on, the fire will lick and spark and pop, and we will see that there was never any "me" besides the sanctioned and endorsed me.

Recently, I read further in that Isaiah passage. I wondered what came after the part she sent me. What did it say after the prophet told the people, from God, that they could walk through the fire, and they would emerge.

Here is what comes next:

> For I am the LORD your God,
>   the Holy One of Israel, your Savior;
> I give Egypt for your ransom,
>   Cush and Seba in your stead.
> Since you are precious and honored in my sight,
>   and *because I love you,*
> I will give people in exchange for you,
>   nations in exchange for your life.[2]

It is as if God is saying to me, *Surrender all your rescue efforts. Walk into the fire and be purified. You will emerge truer. You will begin to actually trust me, because you will finally see that the fuel in the fire is love.*

I love you too much to let you settle for approval. It's not enough. You were made for more. Burn it down. I promise the love-fueled fire will not set you ablaze, will not consume you.

Approval is fine, but it's never going to deliver. Not in the way I need it to, anyway. Approval will never be able to convince me that I'm the kind of girl who gets love.

I don't believe it. Not yet, anyway. It all sounds good, and reads well, and preaches, but I'm not sure it's in my skin yet. So the only thing I know to do is to open up, to begin. And then do it again.

So I'll sit with these prophetic lines from Isaiah until enough of my too-tight skin has been removed and love can seep in.

● ● ●

fourteen

This Is the Work We Are Doing

Make me brave. Lead me into the enormous
space of becoming.

Sue Monk Kidd

On the last day of the kids' two-week spring break, after we had
been to the Colorado River with friends and to Tahoe to visit family—after we had received and then blessed others with the gift of
the stomach flu and finally returned home healthy-ish—I suspended
chores and logistics and the digging out, and the kids and I went to
the beach instead. I took a video for Steve, who was still away, but
then consciously put my phone in my bag and watched them dig
for clams like it was their job, working feverishly with their heads
down, crouched, inspecting the sand.

115

When we arrived, it was morning, and the cloud cover was gray and damp. The kids took plastic cups down to the water's edge and made tiny clam aquariums until the sun burned off the marine layer. Then they all three took the yellow boogie board into the water and caught little shore sets until they were shriveled and shivering. They ran to my blanket and they buried each other in the warm sand.

I chain-chewed at least eight pieces of cinnamon gum, one after another after another, and I drank three sparkling waters in a row, one after another after another. I was anxious, and my desperate desire to want to be present and enjoy the moment made me more anxious.

I decided I would not punish myself—I would not hold hostility toward myself—for being fidgety and compulsive. I would just sit there and breathe. Breathe in, hold it in, breathe out, hold it out, just like Lane taught me. She learned this "square breathing" technique at school, and it is coming in very handy on the beach.

Breathing opens me up when anxiety wants to close me down, and I am a bit more able to take in the salt and the sand and the sound of the barking gulls. I stayed with myself, like a buddy. On the way home, we inched through the In-and-Out drive-thru line and ate our burgers as we continued east.

I remember going to the beach as a child and we would stay at the beach for hours, under the marine layer, playing and chilled. And then we'd drive east, and we'd run to the backyard and jump in the pool because it was hot-hot once you drove those twenty-five minutes east and left the insulation of that cloud cover.

We'd pull in our driveway and peel off our sweatshirts and towels and greet the twenty-degree swing.

The kids and I pull into our driveway after I have watched the temperature gauge slowly rise the entire way home. We step out of the car into hot light.

The kids cannonball into the pool before I put them each in my shower, rinsing sand from every nook and cranny. While the other two are getting dressed, I put Lane on a step stool in front of my mirror and begin working the leave-in conditioner through her thick, wavy, unruly hair while she stares at herself.

I begin brushing her wet hair, as gently as I can because she shrieks like a cat if I don't, and then I turn the blow dryer on high. I run the brush through her hair, following it with the dryer, shaking out the excess water in the next section.

Her brown hair gains a copper sheen as it dries.

I look, alternately, from my work with the brush to her reflection in the mirror. She is inspecting my work, turning her head from side to side to see how smooth her hair has become. She's pleased. I can tell. We smile at each other in the mirror.

I am there. I am there for all of it.

Five days later, I took the kids to the pediatrician for their annual well-child checkups, and when the doctor checked Luke's ears, she said, "I think you've been to the beach. I can see a few pieces of sand in your ears!" She reported the same findings in Lane's and Elle's ears too.

We all giggled. Remains of the day. Traces of adventure. Totally (extra)ordinary. Sand in the ears.

As our inner life feels tight and restrictive, we go looking for ways to broaden it externally. As our inner life expands and we begin to come home to ourselves, we do not need the pace and proving and productivity of the external life like we once did.

It keeps calling me: a slightly smaller external life, and a slightly larger interior life.

Tending—directing one's mind and energies toward, literally stretching toward, to pay attention—is the ritual of beginning again, and it is impossible to tend when we are frantic. So when I feel this longing to tend to Lane's scrambled hair and I notice the color changing as I dry it, I know something has almost imperceptibly begun shifting.

I am not running circles around my life, trying to make it all better. I'm standing in the middle of it. And I know I am where I belong.

On the mornings when I do get up and I feel threatened or self-loathing or trapped, I know what I have to do. I have to stop. If I live, move, and have my being from that cornered place, whatever I do will not actually be life. It will be quivering chickens.

So I must stop. Look at that scared, wild-eyed girl and pick her up in my arms and carry her directly back to God. Here she is. Please love her and keep her and nourish her. I do not have what she needs. I cannot meet the vastness of her need. Please hold her. She's extra scared today. She's chewing gum like a maniac. She's the loudest voice in my head right now and I need help comforting her. Can you hold her, God? Can you hold her for me?

I need to begin again.

When we run circles around our lives, trying to prove we have what it takes, we are simply reinventing the law. We are saying, thank you for grace, but I would rather live by the law. I don't have time to stand here and brush my daughter's hair! I've got to do something that matters with my life!

118

I would rather work hard and earn my worth and be sure I am doing something that matters. I would rather keep score because it brings me some kind of comfort. I would rather live on my own merit. I'd rather secure my own success. Waiting for the wind of the Spirit is too nebulous for me. Trusting that everything I'm trying to secure for myself, I already have . . . well, that's just not possible. I've got to hustle and prove and strive my way into significance.

And, on top of all that, I've got to fix fix fix.

Of course. This was our original temptation: If you *do* this (eat the apple), you will *be* limitless. Our doing got hooked to our being, and the work we are now doing is to surrender that connection.

This is the work we are doing.

Do you know what grace is? Grace is this: you have nothing to prove. Can you even imagine? You have nothing to prove. You have nothing to prove. You have nothing to prove.

You are held, just as you are.

Your only work is to begin again and again with the invitation. We walk to the table at 5 a.m. We open our hands. God invites. We respond. Everything we do, everything we attempt, everything everything everything flows out of that place.

To begin again, then, is not to buy into this system with its try-harder, do-better, get-it-together culture. To begin again is to realize you are actually living in a completely different system altogether. Already. You have been jumping through one unnecessary hoop after another and it's possible to just stop. Stand still. Be still and know, deep down—further down in a place inside you that hardly has words—that you are part of a different system.

Aha.

Your system, the system you are standing directly in the middle of already, is not majoring on who does what right or wrong and when. This just isn't the language of your system. Your system is transcendent. It is not rooted in human control or human behavior. It is a system rooted in God loving us, no matter what. And if we will stand still long enough to realize it, we will see that the God-love system flipped everything around and tells us that it is not up to us to get it right, whatever that means. It is time for us to simply open our ears to the Voice of Love and listen for the next invitation. In other words, join the flow.

> Through the Spirit, Christ offered himself as an unblemished sacrifice, freeing us from all those dead-end efforts to make ourselves respectable, so that we can live all out for God.[1]

You mean I am warrior and wounded and it's OK? I'm loved for being wounded as much as I am for being warrior? And the warrior part of me has gifts for the wounded part of me, but the wounded also has gifts for the warrior? You mean my scars, my limp, might be the most soulful thing about me, not my slick competence?

I heard someone say recently that when we begin to gain liberation, when we begin to unhook our worth and our meaning from what we produce and how "good" we are, those who are still locked in this system, those who are not-yet-free, will be deeply bothered by our audacity. Even unknowingly, they will come after us, because we have broken the understood rules of the tribe.

120

We are no longer trading our effort and energy for love. Somehow, by the grace of God, we got it. We found out the good news that we are OK and we are loved no matter what. *Nothing can separate us from the love of God.*[2] But those who haven't yet ingested that good news are tied up and chained, and when they see us leaving the merit system that we are all supposed to be living by, earning, earning, earning, well, they don't like it that someone else may have found another way. We are breaking the understood rules.

This is where the spiritual discipline of disappointing people really shines. We begin to see that we cannot follow God's invitation of liberation for us and also please everyone. It's just not possible. Some days we will get up and we will live fully out of the knowledge we are loved and "in" no matter what, and we will let the chips fall where they may. Other

So, *this*, my friends, is the work we are doing . . . whatever it takes to stay put and allow ourselves to be held.

days, we will scamper around like a spooked colt, trying to fit in everyone's boxes for us. And then we will tire, and realize we must begin again. We are running around our lives instead of standing in the middle of them.

So, *this*, my friends, is the work we are doing . . . whatever it takes to stay put and allow ourselves to be held.

This is the work we are doing . . . making the following our minute-by-minute mantra:

We will not compare ourselves with each other as if one of us were better and another worse. We have far more interesting things to do with our lives. Each of us is an original.[3]

121

This is the work we are doing . . . getting sand in our ears, making clam aquariums, shampooing sandy scalps, brushing out bobbed hair, standing still.

This is the work we are doing . . . releasing our image and re-membering our identity.

● ● ●

fifteen

Speak Louder

And I'll be the poet who sings your glory—
and live what I sing every day.

Psalm 61:8

I was sitting in church weeks ago. I was feeling triggered and dis-
couraged about my work—feeling like I either had to sell my soul
to the marketing gods or go write near a pond in a remote forest
in total anonymity.

This is that entirely unhelpful, do-or-die, dualistic thinking.

So I was sitting in church and I was in knots. And I cannot even
tell you what the sermon was about that morning, because God
was whispering in my ear to read the parable of the talents. "Get
out your phone, Leeana, and read the parable of the talents. And
read it in The Message translation. Right now."

The voice wasn't panicked; it was direct.

So I did.

I dug my phone out of my purse and I pulled up the parable of the talents in The Message and I started reading. I completely checked out of anything else happening in the room, and I read a story I have read at least a hundred times in my life.

This time, though, it was new.

If you're familiar with the story, you know that the master needs to leave on a trip, and he wants to give his servants some money so they can invest it while he's gone and keep his business flourishing. He gives one servant $5,000. Another servant gets $2,000. And then the third gets $1,000.

The first servant goes out and doubles the money. The second servant does the same. The third servant "dug a hole and carefully buried his master's money."

After some time, the master returns and he checks in with his servants to see what they've done with the money he left in their care. The first servant produces $10,000. "Good work! You did your job well. From now on be my partner," the master says. The second servant produces $4,000. "Good work! You did your job well. From now on be my partner," the master says.

And the third servant says the following: "I was afraid I might disappoint you, so I found a good hiding place and secured your money. Here it is, safe and sound down to the last cent."[1]

I read it again and again and these were the words that stood out to me:

Afraid.

Disappoint.

Good hiding place.

When we are operating out of fear—when we are afraid to be a disappointment—the whole mission gets distorted. We fall into the lie that it is better to hide and protect than to honor and risk.

We clutch at something that was only, always meant to be given away.

As the story goes, the master is furious. He says, "That's a terrible way to live! It's criminal to live cautiously like that! If you knew I was after the best, why did you do less than the least?" He goes on to call this third servant a "'play-it-safe' who won't go out on a limb." He then says, "Throw him out into utter darkness."[2]

For most of my life I've read this story with some kind of pressure attached to it. Like, you better make something of yourself and what God's given you. You better not make God mad. You better not disappoint him.

On that Sunday, weeks ago, in church, I read it differently. Or it rested in my soul differently. I saw how, when fear is our motivator, it blocks us and congests us and stunts us. It keeps us from expanding into the God-ordained space we have been invited to take up in this world.

Our fear response as humans is to hide. Always has been. And so for those of us who struggle like this, we make a lot of excuses about why we can't go for it, why we are unwilling or unable to live the life we've been invited (and gifted) to live.

God has opened up spaces in my life. He has cleared a path for me and has provided opportunity. He's given me certain resources, talents. He's done that for you too. I can bury that opportunity out of fear that I'll mess it all up. Or, I can open my hands and give away what he's given to me.

I can practice expanding. Showing up. Using my voice. Trusting my instincts. Taking a risk. Making an investment . . . even if that investment is in me.

We do not take this on as a mantle of worry and fear and pressure bearing down on us. God's expectations of us are not crushing. What I take from this story is that God accounts for failure. It's going to be part of the gig. But what irks him is when we bury what he's given us. When we find a "good hiding place," thinking we're doing him a favor by protecting his investment. This was never the plan.

The plan was to let it ride and see what happens.

I secretly believed I would experience a level of approval that would confirm I was doing the right thing. Wouldn't that make it easy? An external confirmation that we're on the right track? I could just play small until that affirmation showed up, but God began surgically addressing my self-sabotage.

What do you want that you're afraid of having, Leeana?

The only person in your way, Leeana, is you. You are afraid that getting what you want will cost you what you have, and that feels like you are caught again. What if there is a third way that I could cut through the landscape of all this?

Ultimately, you need to confront your control. Once again, I'm asking you to stop running and turn and look at what you are so afraid of. Let's look at it for what it is. Again, the small injured part of you cannot withstand exposure. She is covering and hovering and posturing and she is so very worried about what everyone is thinking of her. She is aware of how many and whose eyes are on her. She is deeply self-conscious. She is deeply image-conscious. She is

126

painfully, acutely aware of who is watching. This is something you can actually leave behind.

It's habit more than it's helpful.

You are in your own way, Leeana, and we have to confront that. In every place where you're blocking your own progress, we have to root that out. With compassion. And this is one of those places. Big time. Do you feel your anxiety and hesitance and confusion and all the swirling? That's an indication you're afraid of getting what you really want.

Let's stop, and begin again.

I find it curious that the master's response to the servant is to have him thrown into "utter darkness." He chose fear instead of freedom, and living out of fear leaves us in the dark.

This is not the work we are doing.

Expansion is not about hustling our way out into the world, scratching and climbing out of an anxious need for upward mobility. Expansion is about our becoming. It is about God carving out a place for us in this world and we decide we will step into that place. Wholeheartedly. Unapologetically.

Some of us are only filling out about one-eighth of the space God has offered us in the world. Some of us are trying to fill out someone else's space. Some of us are refusing to set foot in the place he has made for us, because we are afraid of how we'll be perceived, afraid of failure, afraid God got it wrong this time.

Believe me. I get it.

I spent some time with a group of women recently, doing the sacred work of waking up some of the most beautiful parts of ourselves that had gone dormant for one reason or another. Sometimes dormancy just happens. It is the result and natural outcome of the seasonality of life. For example, during the early years of mothering, parts of ourselves quiet. It is just what happens when you are learning—for the first time—to care entirely for another human being while trying to maintain some kind of care for yourself.

Most of us, when we are learning something brand new, simply cannot hold enough space for all we are experiencing.

Or if you go through a protracted season of grief or a mental health flare-up, it is impossible to keep all the most vibrant parts of you online. They must rest while you are recovering.

But then there comes that season, that day, that hour, when it is time to do the holy and sacred work of going back in and waking them up again. Reconnecting with those pieces and parts of ourselves that we are now ready to explore, and that we have a sense will serve us going forward.

What we find, which is so interesting, is that we are both returning to a part of us that has always been there, and we are also experiencing that part of us anew. We realize that we are not superhuman, and when we try to be, we end up feeling subhuman—neither of which is our God-given identity.

In the process we discover . . .

It's really hard to authentically respond to God's invitation while we're trying to protect ourselves and our image at the same time.

We cannot trust God and be in control at the same time.

We will not experience true freedom as long as we are trying to outrun our fears.

On my fortieth birthday, my dear friend Wanida slid a little black box across the table to me. Wanida has the spiritual gift of "Giving MAC Makeup." Not sure if you've heard of this one. I think there's an obscure reference to it somewhere in the New Testament. Anyway, Wanida slid this slick black lipstick box to me across the table. I opened it and twisted the tube to reveal a gorgeous shade of hot pink. I winked at her, as she knows I love this color. But that wasn't it. She winked back and motioned to me to turn it over and see the name of the lipstick color.

I flipped the tube on its end and these words were looking back at me:

SPEAK LOUDER

In all caps. My eyes filled and Wanida said, "Speak louder. We need to hear your voice."

I knew what she meant, and it wasn't about volume. She meant, don't be that guy who buried it all because of the fear of being a disappointment. She was saying, "Let it ride, and let's see what happens."

● ● ●

sixteen

Around My Neck

Let love and faithfulness never leave you;
bind them around your neck,
write them on the tablet of your heart.

Proverbs 3:3 NIV

It is Mother's Day, and I am considering my options since Steve is still away. I'm trying to think back to what we did for my mom growing up, a single mom on Mother's Day. Did we take her out? Did we buy her gifts? I can't remember for sure. It's strange to plan a party in your own honor, but it's also strange to let the day pass.

I decided I would take the kids to do something I had been wanting to do, but first we *had* to get the oil changed in the minivan. I had put it off long enough and I didn't want to make the long-ish drive we were about to embark on with the worry that the engine would blow at any minute. Turns out—great news—Jiffy Lube is pretty quiet on Mother's Day.

After the relief of car maintenance, we will drive northwest to a Benedictine monastery up the coast. St. Benedict is, of course, the father of this sacred sentence, "Always we begin again," that walks with me, and I have been feeling the magnetic pull to go visit. I am not Catholic, and it has been many, many years since I've attended mass, but we will go because I want to inhabit this sentence. I want to get closer to it, and its way of life.

I tell the kids about the abbey, who lives there, and why. "Like Maria and the abbey in 'Sound of Music'?" they ask. "Yes," I say, but explain that this abbey is for men. They are very curious about men in robes.

We begin our pilgrimage, on our way to pay homage, and Lane and Elle immediately start fighting over a stuffed pink poodle directly behind me. I say, louder than I mean to, "Stop fighting!" and I pull the car over to the side of the road because I can feel my pulse rising and sweat forming in the small of my back. I just keep breathing. Saying nothing. The kids are quiet. When I'm calmer, I pull back onto the road and get on the freeway.

When we arrive, mass is in progress, and we sit down in the folded chairs that have been added outside as overflow seating, filling the walkway right outside the huge stained-glass doors of the Abbey Church.

In no time my kids are up out of their seats, joining a tribe of kids already playing in the large grass lawn and rock paths behind me. Funny how kids who do not know each other can instantly find a game to play, especially if it means they do not have to sit still for the mass.

131

I am trying to hear the liturgy, the homily, but the wind is blustery and rattling the leaves on the maple tree behind us, and so I can only hear every few words or so. I'm trying to decide if this is frustrating me or not. The ocean is a few miles away and you can feel the soft, balmy air coming off the water and rising up the hill where we're trying to hear. I keep turning around because the rustling of the leaves is so loud I can't believe it's really from the wind.

Since I couldn't hear much of what was being said from the front of the sanctuary, my eyes found the huge stained-glass doors, propped open so those of us in overflow could see. Inscribed in the stained glass was *kyrie eleison*, "Lord, have mercy," which is said to be uttered as an expression of affirming God's love.

Lane runs up to me, drops a bouquet of small purple-and-white flowers into my hands—flowers she's presumably picked illicitly from somewhere—and she scampers off to return to the game.

As mass ends, my kids make a beeline for the cookie table in the guest center. They eat snickerdoodles and the girls sip coffee and find an old man with an old dog to talk to. A woman with a million keys opens the door to the gift shop, which is there in the guest center as well, and I follow her in.

I decided I would get myself a Mother's Day gift: a St. Benedict medal that I'd wear around my neck so as, like Proverbs tells us, to never let love and faithfulness leave me.[1] Especially the love and faithfulness found in the mercies-are-new-every-morning of beginning again. Bind them around my neck.

I gave the shopkeeper my $14 and tucked my (semi-)precious purchase into my purse. We walked over to a garden area containing the Stations of the Cross where we could see beyond the crosses to the Pacific Ocean, baby blue in the distance. In the garden, the kids found the largest snail I have ever seen in my life and, now hyper from the cookies, were threatening each other with its ooze. Things were starting to decline. Time to drive back down to East County and tuck into our favorite sushi restaurant before the Mother's Day crowds hit.

As we walked from the Cross garden to the parking lot, we passed a huge statue of Jesus, arms open, welcoming guests. Luke said, "That would be the perfect spot for a fountain, Mom." I couldn't argue, though I liked making eye contact with Jesus as we walked by. I had wanted to see the black Madonna and the entire sanctuary. I had wanted to talk with one of the monks for longer than the few pleasantries we exchanged when he handed me a Mother's Day rose. I had wanted to be bathed in the Benedictine Rule. Alas. I got to see Jesus, his arms spread wide open to me, the breeze across my face. As I herded three hopped-up kids past him, I could have sworn he winked at me.

Later that evening, after sushi in the sun and a nap and a game of Sorry with Elle, I took out my new medal—gold and silver, a picture of St. Benedict on one side, a cross on the other, and a small loop at the top to string it on a chain. I spent some time remembering back to where I was, over nine years ago, when St. Benedict's sentence found me. I was nursing two babies in a condo by the coast, and I kept thinking, "If this is all I ever wanted, why is it so hard?"

I would give anything to go back and tell myself how beautiful I was, what an attentive and nurturing mother I was, to help myself through, or just to hold my own hand.

Why are the things that matter most in life so hard? Such beautiful burdens? With every beginning comes some kind of ending, and endings often hurt.

Wriggling out of tension feels so good—alleviating the pressure no matter what it costs. I am tempted in a hundred different ways to squirm out of the agitation in my own life. I want to believe this is human nature. We are wired to resist pain. But "God does not waste pain," my friend Linsey said recently. "He is into upcycling." I think that's true, though I don't have to like it. Luckily, our image-bearing soul cannot be crushed in the same way other parts of us can. It can't be wrecked—by us or by others. It's that part of us that God "created . . . godlike, reflecting God's nature,"[2] so pain only serves to wake it up, if we will allow ourselves to awaken to the discomfort instead of dulling it.

We are allowed to escape. We are given that freedom. But those who have sat in the discomfort and listened and waited know that an even deeper freedom awaits those who will *discern an ending* instead of *devise an escape*.

Escapes are almost never in our best interest (unless we're talking about a burning building or an abusive relationship). Endings are about surrender. Escapes are about control. Discernment is belabored and holy work. Devising is quick-fix territory.

We probably already had an inkling of where our journey was headed. We knew we were on an unsustainable ride. We just weren't ready to see. We just hadn't fully embraced the knowing. We needed the time in the darkness. And it's all OK, I'm learning. It's our process. It's our process of not just accepting our circumstances but accepting our humanity and all the glorious limitations that accompany being human.

Here's what it means to be human: I cannot see everything, I cannot know everything, I cannot be awake to everything. And it's OK. It doesn't mean I'm lost or worthless. It means I will forever be in need of God, of a guide (or two), of a great cloud of witnesses (in Target), of coffee at the kitchen table at 5 a.m. (also known as "waiting for faraway things"), of surrendering to the invitation—even if it doesn't all make perfect sense (see the entire story of Gideon).

We're still trying to decide, each and every day, if God can be trusted. We're still beginning again most days, because we get our grubby hands back on our own lives, and then we see that we have no real big winning ideas without being connected to the Source.

The way we forgive ourselves, hang in there with ourselves, grieve and celebrate in the same breath is to . . . begin again. This is the simplest and most profound truth I come back to.

We love the idea of doing things once and for all, but this is not where meaning is found. We don't take communion once and for all. We don't love our spouse once and for all. We don't parent once and for all. We don't do the dishes or the laundry or the vacuuming once and for all. We don't read, endure the commute, or shave our legs once and for all.

We return—in what becomes a sacred connection—to the mundane task, to the moment. And then we do it again. Over and over. Again. This is the raw material of our living. And none of it is to be overlooked.

This is not insanity or hilarity or nuisance or idiocy. This is the task of humanity. To return. To reinvest. To breathe. To begin again. The focus is on the process, the participation, not the product. Ever.

The agitation gets our attention like comfort can't. We hit the wall, but maybe this time, we see the door, we cross the threshold, we step through. We get to see the life that's waiting for us on the other side of surrender.

Yes, Lord have mercy on us, with our bickering kids and overdue oil changes and our limping marriages and our demanding responsibilities and all our strained circumstances and small seeds of hope that we are holding out to you, asking you to grow. Are you there? Can you hear us? Can you help us?

The wind is still whipping around today. Blustery and busy and noisy in all the trees. Perhaps this wind in the trees was to be the homily all along—louder and more poignant than words. *Yes*, it says, *I am here*.

• • •

Part 4

On the
Other Side of
Surrender

seventeen

To Give Back

I'm sitting at my kitchen table, reading a story I don't like. I've always thought this story was brutish and awful, in fact It's the story of God telling Abraham to take his beloved son, Isaac, up to a mountain in Moriah and sacrifice him as a burnt offering.

I'm sorry, what?

Abraham does it. He tells Isaac that they are going to offer a sacrifice to God in worship together. So they, along with two servants and a donkey, begin the journey to Moriah and up the mountain. At a certain point Abraham tells his servants to stay behind, as he and Isaac would proceed alone. Isaac notices that his dad has brought along wood, flint, and a knife. "Where is the sheep for the burnt offering, Dad?" Isaac asks Abraham.

"God will provide the sheep," Abraham tells Isaac. And when they get to the place God had directed them, Abraham begins building an altar. And then, the story tells us, he ties Isaac to the altar, and takes his knife to Isaac's throat.

It is at this absolute eleventh hour that God intervenes, stopping Abraham from taking his own son's life. In the thicket nearby, a ram was entangled, and Abraham releases Isaac, and instead, they kill the ram and offer it as the burnt sacrifice in worship to God.[1]

It seems so cruel and macabre. Why would God make such an appalling request of Abraham? Is this who God is? And, what in the world does this have to do with us today, in the land beyond burnt animal (or human, for that matter) sacrifices?

On closer inspection, and this is important, there is one sentence in the text that is incredibly curious. When Abraham tells his servants to stay back, he also says this: "Stay here with the donkey. The boy and I are going over there to worship; then **we'll** come back to you."[2]

Abraham tells the servants that "we" will come back to you, meaning him and Isaac.

Abraham already knew he would be bringing Isaac back down the mountain with him; he already knew he would not have to kill him.

God asked him to climb the mountain and put a knife to his son's throat, and yet Abraham knew God would provide a substitute and would not allow him to go through with sacrificing his son.

So was this some sort of divine game of chicken that Abraham assumed he had the stomach to win?

I wonder if Abraham knew, in his bones, what we are all trying to learn: that with God, every wall is a door. What we, in our limited human perception, see as an ending, is likely just a beginning. I wonder if Abraham already knew the answer to one of our greatest questions: Is God a giver or is God a taker? He knew, regardless of the circumstances, that God was a good giver and not a maniacal taker. In other words, God had a plan, as he always does. But the plan, as it always does, required surrender.

The word *surrender* traditionally means "to give up," which feels a bit like quitting or resigning or escaping, and so the idea of surrender can almost feel passive or like failure. But I came across another meaning of the word *surrender*: "to give back." Giving back, which feels slightly different than giving up, reminds me of God's words to me— God's profoundly healing words "Bring her to me."

> **Surrender begets surrender, because we see—once we tolerate the invitation—that it is in our best interest.**

I did not want to hand God the most precious, precarious part of me. And yet, I could see that even in my best intentions of caretaking and comforting, I was drowning in her needs. Bringing her back to God, again and again, has also helped me open my hands in my marriage, with my kids, and in my work. Surrender begets surrender, because we see—once we tolerate the invitation—that it is in our best interest.

Everything we are, everything we have, God has given to us. Freely and without strings attached. We get to do with it whatever we want. Our gifts, our relationships, our callings, our time, our resources, our very breath. Is God asking us to put a knife to the throat of all we love? Not literally, no. But over and over and over again he asks us to give back to him, open up, so that he can give us more.

When God stops Abraham's hand from injuring Isaac, he also tells Abraham that he will give him descendants that outnumber the stars in the sky, the grains of sand on the beach. When Abraham chooses to give back to God that which is most precious to him, his hands were then open to receive more.

Is God inviting you toward what you perceive to be a wall, an ending? If so, could you hold space for the possibility that this wall may, on closer inspection, become a door into all of eternity — something bigger and more transcendent than you can imagine?

I'm walking with you up the mountain and asking you to give me back the very thing you do not want to give. But that is never the end of the story. When I am asking you to give something back to me, it is because I want to give back to you a thousandfold.

> You're blessed when you stay on course,
>   walking steadily on the road revealed by God.[3]

Beginning again — whether in the smallest moment or the largest — usually requires us to put something on the altar. Our ego. Our resentments. Our regrets. Our anger. Our fear. Our dreams. Our past, present, future. Our beloveds. Most of all, perhaps, beginning again requires we put our narratives of scarcity on the altar. We get stuck because we refuse to believe in the reality of abundance or the possibility that abundance could be for us and not just for everyone else.

The mark of beginning-again spirituality is abundance. We surrender because we trust, somewhere deep down, that God is a giver and not just a taker. He has more—not less—for us.

More freedom.

More forgiveness.

More joy.

More peace.

More love.

More patience.

More hope.

More desire.

More intimacy.

More vulnerability.

More. Not less.

Scarcity tells us to clutch, desperately, to life. Even if it's half life. Abundance says, *It's OK to open up; you will not be consumed.*

Yes, maybe God is asking you to place something unthinkably precious on the altar. But like the cross, the altar isn't the final resting place of the story.

Life, new life, is the story. What we thought was a wall might be a door . . . is the story. Beginning again—especially after the darkness of death—is the story. Because what is waiting for us, if we will moment by moment believe, is more.

And to those of us who cannot, yet, put our scarcity on the altar and give it back to God, we are as loved and as held as ever. He will always be inviting us to Moriah, up the mountain, so that he can provide a ram in the thicket and descendants galore. But if we cannot go, if we cannot climb, if we cannot stack the sticks or strike the flint, he will not curse us.

And yet, he will never stop calling.

Always, though, we get to decide. Will we clutch, self-protect, control? Or will we give back to God what we have—however beautiful or broken—so that he might be able to fill the sky of our lives with something we cannot yet see?

● ● ●

eighteen

I Become Myself

Because the woman I love lives inside of you . . .

Hafiz

Last December, I was asking God to give me a transcendent moment in the midst of what felt like a bit of madness. Four of the five members of our little family have December birthdays, and the month always tends to be a push-pull for me, doing my best to be present and also attend to what feels like one million tiny details and desires.

I asked God to bring me something transcendent that would lift me above the logistics and above all of Steve's coming and going for work. Something that would relieve me, momentarily, of all the beautiful burdens and give me a glimpse of God himself.

I looked for a concert, a performance, an activity that would transport me. And nothing arrived. Then, on December 8, I had my last speaking engagement of the year. I drove up to a north county coastal town wearing my red velvet jacket, and God whispered in my ear: *Leeana, be generous. Be generous in your offering to these women.*

I asked God to help me. And I got up and spoke, giving away my stories, my empathy, my hope, my tears, my heart, my dumb jokes. I gave it all away. And as I was placing my little life in God's hands that December morning, I got the chills under my red velvet jacket, because what I realized, even as I was speaking to this roomful of women, was that my transcendent moment was happening right then.

I knew, even as I stood there with a mic in my uncertain hand, that I was receiving what I had longed for in the very moment I was giving myself away.

No one was more surprised than me. I thought I'd be listening to beautiful music or hearing a truly inspired sermon. I thought I'd read a piece on advent that would move my heart or hear a podcast that brought me to tears. I had not considered that I would be given such a gift in the very moment that I was offering.

I thought I'd be in the stands. Instead, I was on the stage. I didn't know what to do with this. Until I saw what God has been saying all along: *When you step into the light, you will see yourself and you will see Me, and you will see others as you never have before. Everyone's place to stand in the light is different. But you will know it when you begin to inhabit your place. And you will be met and held in ways that will transcend yourself.*

"Perhaps creating something," the poet Rilke writes, "is nothing but an act of profound remembrance."[1] When we offer our creating to God—whatever that looks like in our own lives—we remember who we are and who he is. We remember that we are the Beloved Creation and that we are held. We remember that we are to take our place in the creation story. We remember that we were made to pour out. We were made to give ourselves back to him; this is how we find ourselves.

> Then Jesus went to work on his disciples. "Anyone who intends to come with me has to let me lead. You're not in the driver's seat; I am. Don't run from suffering; embrace it. Follow me and I'll show you how. Self-help is no help at all. Self-sacrifice is the way, my way, to finding yourself, your true self. What kind of deal is it to get everything you want but lose yourself? What could you ever trade your soul for?"[2]

When I can sink into the knowledge that it's his breath, his *pneuma*, in my lungs, I am emboldened. The channel is freer, less blocked, and what pours out is generous and free flowing, less self-conscious. When I become my distorted peacock self, overly worried about outcomes, the words get stuck as they come up and out of my mouth.

You and I were made to participate in something beyond ourselves, to be instruments of God's peace, to be bridges over troubled waters. *Self-sacrifice is the way, my way, to finding yourself, your true self.*

Other translations of this verse say that we are to "deny ourselves, take up our cross, and follow Jesus." I think this word "deny" has been so misused. Some of us have been taught or have believed that denying ourselves means abandoning ourselves, and by no means are these two the same thing.

Abandoning ourselves is resignation, repression, bullying.

Denying ourselves means listening to the transcendent voice and following the transcendent way instead of listening to the toxic inner voices of fear and control.

We are invited to deny all those empty props and false promises, so we can get down to the real business at hand. We surrender ourselves and all our big plans, which is different than silencing ourselves, sidelining ourselves.

Surrender, throughout Scripture, is not something someone else can come and take from us. It's something only we can give. An act of submission. And yet, listening to that Inner Voice of Love brings us closer to, not farther away from, who we were created to be. We bring God these broken, wounded, bruised parts of ourselves. We bring God these puffed-up, "successful," praised parts of ourselves. And we put it all in his hands. The parts of us we have worked so hard to become. The parts of us we have rejected so entirely. The bloated and the broken. We give it all to him and let him show us what remains.

When he begins to reveal the gold in us, we must never again abandon that gold. We must never again mute it, silence it, reject it, believe it is not enough. We must, every single day—again and again—ask God to give us the wisdom to honor the gold. And we must always remember that, in order to honor the gold, we will have to deny the dross. We will not do this once and for all; we will do this like a practice.

Exhibit A:

I bought a flight suit. I know. Weird.

I had seen the flight suit at a store in the mall and admired it a few times, but I could not find one single reason why purchasing such a garment made any sense whatsoever. So I kept passing it up. And still, over months, I kept thinking about it. Not because I believed it would solve any problems or make me look a certain way or help me feel any more spiritual or because I thought it would deliver my self-esteem to me in a zip-front uni-suit. But just because I wanted to honor the fact that I kept being drawn back to it for some unexplained reason.

So I went to the store in the mall and I tucked myself behind the flowing boho curtain of the dressing room and stepped into the fatigue-green suit.

When he begins to reveal the gold in us, we must never again abandon that gold.

I looked at myself in the mirror and knew immediately I would purchase the flight suit. Here's why: I felt strong and creative in it. And I can't think of two better things to feel. When I put it on and looked in the mirror, somehow it helped me recognize me.

I wasn't sure it was all that flattering or where in the world I would wear it. I wasn't sure there was one shred of practicality to this purchase. Oh well. Sometimes that stuff doesn't matter so much. The flight suit was my way of honoring the gold in me: the wise center, the creativity, my voice.

The purchase was an act of paying attention to and commemorating the woman on the stage, who—sometimes reluctantly and fearfully—shows up and speaks. When I choose to live from her,

149

give to others from her, God always has a way of nodding to me, telling me it is good. I cannot imagine a more worthy act of celebration.

I'm learning to listen, to move from timid to truer, again and again and again.

• • •

nineteen

Maybe There's Not That Much to Do After All

Come to me, all you who are weary and burdened,
and I will give you rest. Take my yoke upon you and learn from
me, for I am gentle and humble in heart, and you will find rest
for your souls. For my yoke is easy and my burden is light.

Matthew 11:28–30 NIV

I wanted to be able to rest without having to be asleep. That's what
I wanted.

I have spent plenty of time in my life sprinting around, frantic and paralyzed all at once, trying, propping, fixing, covering,
patching, controlling, withdrawing . . . and wouldn't you know

that all those efforts produced so much less than I thought they would. God told me in no uncertain terms that I could keep up the dance I was doing. No problem. But he also told me that if I looked closely, I would see that my coping strategies were not actually helping.

And then, he asked if I wanted to stop. Did I want to take a Sabbath from all this trying too hard to keep things going?

All this would require is surrender. Opening up instead of covering up. Over and over again. This seemed like the most impossible invitation until I felt how impossible the agitation was becoming. And I decided I would do this thing: I would stop running. I would stand still and look right into the thing I did not want to look at. I finally realized the not-looking was costing me, and I finally believed that the looking would not consume me.

For the longest time, I had so much to do. Endless tasks. So much of what I was trying to secure, I see now, was actually none of my business. I was trying to create a smooth surface to my life, even when certain areas of my life were anything but smooth, and it was costing me. Costing me honesty. Costing me integration. Costing me wholeness. Costing me freedom. I was serving something that was not serving me, and so I was pouring time and energy and effort into a void.

And now . . . now I feel like maybe there's not that much to do after all.

Just the tending. To tend. Attend. Be in attendance. Present and accounted for.

Tending feels like nothing but tedium when we are striving. But once we have unhanded these very tender places in our lives, we see how tending helps tether us to today. It makes us slow down and participate in the menial and the mundane. Right here. And when I am hustling and striving and trying to hold things together, tending is one of the last things on my list, *because it requires me to let the moment fall open.* And I feel I just don't have the strength to let that happen.

As God has been helping me hold the most agitated parts of me, tending feels more possible. And more than that, I feel drawn—by the soul voice—to the raised bed in the yard, the brush and Lane's wild mane, the hall closet, the prep for the chimichurri sauce, the potted bougainvillea. The voice in my soul invites me to the lemon tree, the rolling hills around my house, the poetry anthology.

This is just unreal, if you ask me, because tending does not yield accomplishment. It's just a practice.

I used to want to put things on a list and cross them off forever. I wanted to arrive once and for all. The thought of beginning again and again of opening up again and again—was impossible, intolerable, and yet I longed for such capacity.

Who has the energy to fight for a marriage day after day, month after month, year after year . . . when things have been hard for so long and the patterns and cycles don't seem to be resolving into health and happiness and ease . . . when everyone's tired and stretched and bouncing off each other?

Who has the energy to begin again with children? To reengage in the same schedule and the same squabbles and the same snacks every day, day after day? Like a run-on sentence. When we know the time is slipping through our fingers and we will want these days back? Who in the world has the determination to give them everything we want to give them when we feel like we don't have anything? How can family life feel like it's evaporating one second and then pond water the next?

Who has the energy to begin again professionally, when the project didn't pan out or the exposure was public or we feel like we're running out of time? Who can get back up and use these feelings of failure and rejection as fuel for something new?

Who has the energy to begin again with life's responsibilities? We write the check this month, knowing we will have to do it all over again the next. We fold the last load of laundry even as the next is piling up. We put all the dishes away even as the next meal is ready to be made. What gives us the capacity to begin again when repetition seems like the most impossible task, like banging your head against a wall instead of movement?

Who has the energy to begin again with her body, which betrays her and yells at her and needs needs needs? Who can stand the inner work required to build a body from the inside out?

And, who has the energy to begin again with herself? To back out of the self-versus-self antagonism and do the very difficult work of treating herself like a companion instead of a critic? Who has the capacity to sit compassionately with herself, over and over again, when all she wants to do is condemn? Who, among us, has the Love within to forgive herself again and again?

Who can open their hurting heart that has clamped shut yet again? Who could let God in once again, even though our faith has not protected us from disappointment, maybe even devastation, maybe even disaster? When we've been burned by people who said they believed too? Who could have the resilience and resolve to go on believing when faith hasn't seemed to produce much of anything? Or so it feels today.

I'll tell you who: none of us.

Some of us are trying. We're trying so hard. We are on our best behavior, implementing our most efficient strategies. We are mastering the art of stamina and we are strong strong strong. We are as capable as they get and we can handle hard things.

But the wall is still coming, and we will never—not one of us—be able to muscle our way through it. God, in his grace, shows us the door, and Love, only LOVE, invites us through.

We bring that wounded, wide-eyed part of ourselves to him—the one we're constantly tempted to appease. We do this over and over and over again. And then, the truth is, there's really not that much to do. We bring him our burden and he gives us rest.

We bring him our burden and he gives us rest.

We got a cat while Steve was away. Moonlight is her name. Lane chose this name because of the black swath across her face, down her back, and up her tail that sits right on top of the white swath that starts on her chin and stretches down her belly.

She's the golden retriever of cats, much to our collective surprise, as aloof as a fur blanket. We rescued her to help us deal with a pesky and unending rat problem. After I had removed a half-dozen or more dead rats from traps, I decided that I would like to seek alternative methods for dealing with this problem.

I called a pest control company and had them out to the house. After a very thorough walk through, I was handed a quote for $1,600 for rat removal. I told my mom this, casually, and the next time she came out from Texas to visit, she brought me an article titled

"Barn Cats." Her point was that people living on farms didn't hire pest control companies to deal with rats; they, instead, shifted the ecosystem.

Enter Moonlight, our two-year-old darling who we are just falling in love with, and no one is more surprised than me. She curls up next to me on the couch, pushing into my side. You could not slip a piece of paper between us. She purrs so loudly I have to turn up *Scandal* to hear it. I scratch her ears and she lays her head in my lap, practically drooling, her eyes rolled back in her head.

I'm watching her and petting her and I realize three things:

1. I have lost track of what's happening on *Scandal*.

2. I have a faint smile on my face.

3. I am awake, and I am at rest.

• • •

twenty

Rituals of Rest

He finds us and saves us from the thieves of our humanity.

Br. Mark Brown

When my twins were first born, and they would miraculously nap simultaneously, I would lie down on the couch with a spoonful of peanut butter in one hand and a Diet Coke in the other and watch reruns of *Dawson's Creek*.

I was in what one might call Survival Mode, and all I could manage was checking out. I don't think this is necessarily evil. I've just come to realize that checking out is not the same thing as real, restorative rest. Real rest brings us back to our center, while checking out takes us far away from ourselves.

Real rest is hard to come by, though, isn't it. Just today I was being shot in the back of the leg with a nerf gun while another child was licking my arm. When life gets overwhelming, all you want to do is RUN to your phone and start lapping up Instagram like it's your next meal.

But at some point, we need to exit Survival Mode—even if it's for an hour or two a week—and learn how to practice the kind of rest that brings us back to ourselves and back to the moment instead of taking us out to sea.

What this has meant for me is relearning what is actually restful to me, and then incorporating those resting practices into my life more regularly. Create a rhythm, so to speak.

Nurturing a healthy life rhythm is about beginning a dialogue with yourself that includes grace, compassion, and a sense of humor instead of the usual ways we deal with ourselves (i.e., contempt, frustration, and disappointment).

This is the kind of conversation you might have with a dear friend. Non-judge-y, genuinely supportive. Except that you're having it with yourself. Because *you are* the dear friend *to you*. (Revolutionary.)

You might say to yourself:

"What would you like to do if you had three hours to yourself? What would be fun, delightful, freeing?"

or

"What do you need today, love? What does your body need? What does your soul need?"

I decided recently that one thing I needed was a skin care regimen. Normally, I am someone who is grossly overzealous about things like skin care, and I buy $300 worth of highly effective serums (I am powerless against the word *serum*). I read the directions and figure out how to use everything I've purchased. But then I begin to obsess about the possibility that perhaps there are other products out there that might be even more effective, and I get sidelined by the worry that I have made the worst possible purchase. By the time I've done all that, I'm exhausted, and I decide to take a baby wipe to my face as I fall into bed.

I determined that skin care was a commitment to tending that I was ready to make, a way I could take radical care of myself, show myself that I could stick to a practice, that I could begin again in one small way, twice a day.

Wash, toner, day cream, eye cream. Makeup. Take off makeup. Wash, toner, night cream, eye cream.

Could I do that for myself? Not because my skin is horrible or I am sick and tired of how puffy my eyes are, but as an act of caretaking, a ritual of rest.

Rest rituals are about determining the things you need in order to, at the very least, function somewhat sanely and, at best, thrive. It might include things you need to do daily, weekly, monthly, quarterly, annually. These are things for your body, your mind, your soul, your hygiene.

One time my husband said to me, during a particularly extended time in the postpartum cave, "Why don't you go to the salon and get your hair . . . cleaned."

Perhaps getting your hair done regularly is something you add to your list of rest-rituals. Maybe it's five minutes of centering breath or meditation. Maybe it's taking a multivitamin every morning or washing your face. Simple practices that help you come back to and tolerate, not numb out, the now. The trick, I've learned, is not so much the actual practice, but actually practicing it.

Here are some examples:

Daily rest: a shower, washing your face, time outside (so good for the mental health), the ritual of coffee or tea time, five minutes of writing, stretching, a dose of beauty

Weekly rest: exercise, making something—soup, a collage, a garden—meeting up with an ongoing group of some kind, doing an activity with your kids that *you* really enjoy

Monthly rest: a visit with a therapist or a spiritual director or counselor, a visit with a safe friend, finishing a good book, a walk in a particularly beautiful place, a babysitter

Quarterly rest: hair appointment, attending a creative workshop, taking a lesson that might enhance one of your hobbies, visiting an inspiring place

Annual rest: a weekend spiritual retreat, a getaway with some girlfriends, a getaway with your partner

This is not a checklist or a to-do list. These are ideas you might want to consider as opportunities for recovery and restoration. Begin by thinking about the things in your life that help you return to you. What are those things?

If you've forgotten, it's OK.

But maybe tonight, after everyone has gone to bed, you could get an old receipt from your wallet and you could smooth it out and turn it over and jot some notes on the back of it about what would help you breathe. Yes, I know going to Paris would help you breathe. I get it. But let's start with something a little more attainable so that we don't totally sabotage ourselves right off the bat.

Once you have a few things written down, consider how those few things might get incorporated into your life . . . daily, weekly, monthly, and so on.

Sometimes we need a spoonful of peanut butter and *Dawson's Creek*. But usually what we're really longing for is living from our center. The etymology of *rest* includes "freedom from toil." Toil isn't just work. Toil is a burden, a slog, a grind. What would bring you freedom—even for an hour—from everything you're carrying?

Think less about pampering and more about a practice.

Regular doses of natural beauty is one of my most essential rituals of rest. Because I've learned this about myself, I pay attention now. For example:

I hadn't seen fireflies in at least two decades, and then just a few weekends ago I was at a cabin in central Virginia, and as twilight descended, tiny Edison bulbs flickered against the fishing pond and the forested gravel road. This is so entirely unlike where I live, in Southern California, where headlights and neon signs replace fireflies.

But there they were, flickering, flirting with us. *Catch me if you can.* My kids could grab them out of the air and watch them inside cupped hands. As night fell, I saw the absolute magic of light flickering, even for a second, in the dark.

The air was thick on our skin and in our lungs, and a croaking frog sounded deeply distressed from his place on the pond bank. The twilight world was loud with life. But all eyes were on the fireflies.

Luke emptied the last of the gallon jug of orange juice into a cup and all eight cousins went about making a habitat. They poked holes in the plastic jug, collected leaves and rocks and sticks. They caught fireflies with their bare hands and deposited them into the jug. Then they shook the jug slightly. Just to jostle the creatures. And the jug lit up like a homemade flashlight.

"It's bioluminescence," Lane said.

She was right, of course—a chemical reaction happening inside those tiny bugs that made them shine. Each time a cousin agitated the orange juice jug, the lights came on.

Each night we waited and waited for enough darkness to descend so that we could see the tiny lanterns floating around us. Each night they did, and it was the most incredible thing I had ever seen.

• • •

twenty-one

Twilight Comes Twice

So here's what I want you to do, God helping you:
Take your everyday, ordinary life—your sleeping, eating, going-to-work, and walking-around life—and place
it before God as an offering. Embracing what God
does for you is the best thing you can do for him.

Romans 12:1–2

I am longing for ordinary, perhaps even experiencing a call to the
ordinary. We have lived in extraordinary for so long—twins, moves
overseas, a baby born in the Middle East, moves back to the States,
deployments. I have always been drawn to big and dramatic and
loud and exciting. And I have never been more ready for ordinary.

In the Christian liturgical calendar, there are two periods called
"Ordinary Time"—a span leading up to Lent and then another

span, which I am in as I write, that stretches from Easter to Advent. This second stretch is called "Trinitytide."

Ordinary Time calls us back to our simple practices, our roots, all our tending that tethers us to the present. Ordinary Time is where we begin again. Not New Year's Resolutions or Lenten Commitments or Advent Waiting. Not the big stuff. Just the ordinary. Feeding the cat. Washing my face. Opening the mail. Reading a poem. Sending a card. Making the meal. Witnessing and being witnessed. Holding. Nourishing and nurturing. I love the idea of the everyday-extraordinary happening in the Ordinary, the periodic elements of this dying-living we are all doing.

Taking our meds. Visiting our guides. Confessing to friends. Breathing. Beginning again. Opening our hands and letting the wilderness—the unknown—be the wild place where new life begins.

This morning, I am back at my kitchen table, in the dark, hot coffee in hand. The heater is cutting through the morning chill. I am reminded, as I type, sip, type, sip, of an idea Beth gave me: that any flat surface can be an altar. She told me that wiping down a countertop or clearing the edge of a bathtub or tidying a desk . . . all of this creates a bit of space that becomes an altar if we will see it that way. A place to commemorate and receive. A place to say thank you and to be loved. A place to surrender.

My prayer at the altar-table is this: God, give me only what I need for today.

I never want this part of my day to end, since starting to practice it. I go to bed looking forward to the heat and the coffee and the darkness. I have worshiped sleep in the past. Wanting rest more than I have wanted anything.

Now, rest is coming. And I am so very held and met in these dark minutes, maybe an hour. I want to harness it, stave off the light, but it comes. The sky begins to change. A child has forgotten to latch the chicken run tightly and the chickens begin moving in my peripheral vision. Important business, those chickens seem to always have, with the ground.

I'm never not surrounded by a stack of books, voices who meet me in this dark pocket. I see how I must get in bed earlier. I must turn the TV off the night before. I must take better care of myself if I am to get up and listen each and every morning.

The decisions to honor this time begin far before 5 a.m., and something about that feels right. Feels congruent. Sacrificial and rewarding, like all worthy things in life. Now on to the altar of the countertop—lunch packing, breakfast making, dish clearing.

Every step an arrival, as the poet Denise Levertov wrote. An arrival into the present, which is always waiting for me to join it.

When I was minutes out of graduate school and brand-newly twenty-four years old, I drove from West Virginia where I had been in school, down to Virginia to pick up my little brother from college, home to San Diego, and then I slept for an entire day. When I woke up, I found a book my mom left on my nightstand. A gift. *Twilight Comes Twice.* It's a children's book about dawn and dusk, a simple reminder that the sun goes down and the sun comes up. Every day. And twice, in between, we get the gift of these golden hours, these pockets of waking up and winding down.

No matter how beautiful and epic and glorious life is right now, the sun goes down. And no matter how ugly and rejecting and hurtful life is right now, the sun comes up. Something about this saved me then and saves me now. I was young and starting over geographically and professionally and relationally. But more than that, the very rhythm of creation was reminding me that it wasn't all up to me. Something was going on that was beyond me, behind me, below me, beside me.

And I just needed to join it, fall into it, beginning again and again and again.

I could join or I could resist. But either way, the sun would set and the sun would rise—with or without me. I could try to outrun the sun with my superhuman striving. I could try to hide in the dark with my subhuman shame. But the invitation, then and now, was to join the rhythm of creation, which is to be what we were simply and profoundly created to be . . . human.

Human. In all its extraordinary everyday ordinary.

If I am failing, stuck, and paralyzed, I always have the opportunity to begin again. And if I am winning, elated, and propelled, I still must begin again. None of us is too far gone, in the same way that none of us has arrived. This is reorienting to the core.

> **Could you and I join the rhythm of twice-a-day twilight that reminds us there are gifts in both the light and dark—illumination and stillness?**

Could you and I join the rhythm of twice-a-day twilight that reminds us there are gifts in both the light and dark—illumination and stillness? If you're in the dark, you can begin again. And if you're in the broad side of the light, you will still need to begin again. This is how we practice being human.

Twilight comes twice.

Yesterday afternoon, as dusk arrived, we were all in the pool, kids climbing on Steve's back and jumping off the diving board in tandem, which I'm absolutely sure is illegal. The kids were screaming their heads off and the water sloshed up and over the sides of the pool from the aftershocks of their dual entries. The setting sun made the pool water glitter like our own personal ocean. And it's hard to imagine a sweeter moment.

But the sun goes down and we come inside and we rest.

And this morning I was up early, and the golden light was back again, the mountains out beyond the kitchen sink window backlit in blush. And I was reminded anew . . .

Whether we are in crisis or chaos or calm, hope or disappointment, burial or resurrection, ordinary or extraordinary, we can—because of the inexhaustible grace of God—begin again.

● ● ●

Epilogue

Practices for Beginning Again

If you are present to the now, and you are
present in love, you are present to God.

Thomas Merton

As you may have picked up by now, I have a love affair with hot pink
bougainvillea. They bloom and billow all over my neighborhood like
brazen women who will not be tamed, and I cannot get enough. In
flower language, bougainvillea represent passion and protection, two
beautiful meanings. But recently I came across another significance:
they are often given to those starting out on a new path in life.

So for those of you who are fresh off failure, staring down a new
normal, living into foreign lands, and/or building from the ground
up, I want to say, me too, I see you, and the bougainvillea on the front
cover are for you. Beauty and brilliance for you as you begin again.

In addition, I wanted to offer you some practices that may serve
as companions along your way. When you are in the midst of an

unexpected beginning or a messy middle in life, it can be tempt-
ing to want to just push ahead to the other side, the ending, where
we assume resolution and peace are waiting for us. I've learned,
though, that we rarely get to this perceived "other side." Instead,
the peace comes when we can sit right where we are.

So I asked some dear friends if they would share the practices
that help them be where they are, help them begin again. Here
is the collective wisdom of some incredible warrior sisters and
brothers. Be blessed.

● ● ●

Release in the Morning: I spend 15 or 20 minutes each morning in a comfy chair in silent prayer, practicing the image in
Psalm 131 "as a stilled and quieted child on its mother's lap is
my soul within me." I sit and let God hold me in silence, and
when I get distracted, worried, start planning the day, I repeat
the word "release" to remind me what I'm doing and open my
intention back to releasing and resting in the Divine embrace.

Release Mid-day: After work, before I hit the ground running
with the family, I have a special journal that I write down a
few lines of anything that I am carrying and need to release
into God's care. Any frustration, worries, to-do's, etc. I end
with the word "release."

Release in the Evening: And every evening I take a bath, again,
same theme, letting my body feel embraced in the warm

water and once again, releasing on a physical level all I've carried and held through the day into the Divine embrace.

-BAS

• • •

Gathering with My Community: What started as a weekly couples Bible study several years ago has become a giant, noisy, kid-overrun family dinner. We laugh, cry, pray, and point one another back to Jesus. To some I'm sure it looks like chaos, but to me, it's life giving and such a sweet time of worship in this season of life.

-HK

• • •

Praying the *Anima Christi* Prayer: When I wake up in the morning and go to bed at night, I lie quietly, taking a few deep breaths, hold my hands over my heart, and recite the *Anima Christi* prayer 1 to 2 times. Slowly, intentionally, sometimes barely audibly. And even when I get distracted, it's OK. I either start over or reflect on a part of the prayer that keeps coming back to me.

Anima Christi Prayer

(Anonymous, early 1300s AD)

Jesus, may all that is you flow into me.
May your body and blood be my food and drink.
May your passion and death be my strength and life.
Jesus, with you by my side, enough has been given.

May the shelter I seek be the shadow of your cross.
Let me not run from the love which you offer, but hold me
safe from the forces of evil.
On all of my dyings shed your light and your love.
And keep calling to me until that day comes when, with
your saints, I may praise you forever. Amen.

-JT

• • •

12 Steps: I read through and pray through the 12 Steps. Surrendering my control, accepting God is God and I am not, asking for help, confession, self-searching, evaluation, service. I breathe slowly and deliberately while reading and praying.

-KM

• • •

Psalm 23 Exercise: When I feel anxious, I like to read Psalm 23, and then I write it out specifically addressing my concerns. For example:

"The Lord is my shepherd, I shall not want"

The Lord will take care of all of my needs today. He will supply food, energy, peace, grace, words, etc. I will lack no thing that I need for today.

"He restores my soul"

He makes me excited about life again . . . giving me new hope and confidence.

-KJ

• • •

The Garden: I wake up early, get a cup of coffee, sit for five minutes with my eyes closed and clear my mind. I envision walking towards a garden and meeting Jesus there and we go inside — just us — before the sun rises. I write a few paragraphs and pray. Then I read Scripture. It's amazing to me that every day He's always standing there waiting for me, holding open the iron door to the garden.

-EM

• • •

Notes of Encouragement: I like to write notes of encouragement to people who have impacted my life in some way (big or small), especially when I'm having a rough day. It helps me remember the ways God has shown me love through people I meet and moments I have experienced something holy.

-JH

• • •

The Welcoming Prayer: Instead of immediately shunning certain thoughts and feelings, sometimes welcoming them in is more effective. I sit with them, acknowledge them even for a moment, and it helps me release even the strongest emotions more easily.

The Welcoming Prayer

(Father Thomas Keating)

Welcome, welcome, welcome. I welcome everything that comes to me today because I know it's for my healing. I welcome all thoughts, feelings, emotions, persons, situations, and conditions. I let go of my desire for power and control. I let go of my desire for affection, esteem, approval and pleasure. I let go of my desire for survival and security. I let go of my desire to change any situation, condition, person or myself. I open to the love and presence of God and God's action within. Amen.

Holding Both: I practice "holding both" instead of forcing myself to agree to either/or. I am both wounded and wonder. I am both soulful and struggling. I am both grateful and exhausted. I am both magic and mundane. I am both empathetic and angry. I am both heartbroken and hopeful.

-LT

• • •

Grounding: I go to the beach once a week and stand in the ocean barefoot. Research shows that "grounding" or "earthing"— keeping our bare feet directly in contact with the ground for 40 minutes—helps us to be more present to our lives and to God's love.

-MS

• • •

Facing East: I get my coffee and sit—either inside or outside— facing East. The sunrise is a gift from God, his faithfulness. I greet the morning and praise God, "This is the day that the Lord has made; let us rejoice and be glad in it." I ask His blessing on my day and the day of my 6 children and 8 grandchildren. And I ask his blessing on my community, my church, my country. Then I read Scripture and use a special highlighter that does not bleed through! This nourishes my soul.

-MM

• • •

Food as Spiritual Practice: Honestly, having the same few things for breakfast every morning has been wonderful as a daily practice to center me for my day. For me it's about having a predictable routine to wake up to each morning, so that I don't have to think about it and can instead connect with my kids and my husband in the busyness of the morning. Also, it helps me be properly fueled, which is the difference between me being a happy mom or a pretty unpleasant person.

-EK

• • •

Practices to Surrender Control:

When I pray, I open my hands, palms up, as a physical expression of surrender.

I sing "He's got the whole world in his hands" and include myself and the people or situations I'm worried about in the song. It is helpful to remember this truth and to bring me back to my childhood trust in God's provision and protection. (Also is fun to do with my kids.)

I walk and notice God in nature, which helps me remember God is present, has not forgotten me and is not worried. He is fully in control.

I think about situations or people I am worried about, picturing myself sitting peacefully on the dock of a lake or river and putting people or situations in fun and safe inner tubes down the river, floating into the loving arms of the Father, Son and Holy Spirit.

-KKJ

• • •

Practicing Boundaries: I am me and you are you and we are each responsible for our own lives and our own feelings. So freeing!

-SS

• • •

Picture It: I read a passage of Scripture in the morning. Then, I take a photo at some point in the day that relates to the passage. It keeps what I read in the forefront of my mind and forces me to really think about it from creative angles to find a way to photograph the concept.

-SJB

• • •

Breath Prayer: The first half of the phrase is to be prayed on the inhale; the second half on the exhale, praying with your breath.

"In Your love, I begin again."

"Breath of life, breathe on me." (by Adele Calhoun)

Apps: The "Pray As You Go" App helps me with contemplative prayer. The "Stop, Breathe & Think App" is a body scan meditation that helps reconnect mind, body, and soul.

-LW

• • •

Writing: It's a release to process thoughts with words that can be deleted or crossed out, yet still placed and seen. It's a release when I'm feeling wounded or excited or lost. As a mom of three young kids and a wife to a busy husband, writing is my place to come alive and feel known, to connect with my centered self and with Jesus

-ET

• • •

Pat My Chest: I do it for a couple reasons, to literally wake my soul up. Stay connected to sacred everyday moments. Remain aware. Remain rooted. I pat my chest to get my soul moving and praising.

Wiggle My Toes: I do it almost involuntarily. It started years ago. Like patting my chest, it's a spiritual awareness thing for me. Keeps me paying attention to what's going on around me. Wakes me up. I wiggle my toes and am instantly reminded "pay attention." Only months ago did a spiritual director tell me "wiggling your toes is a natural way our bodies reset." I was shocked. That's exactly what it's been for me, a reset. She told me that patting my chest is the same thing, it's a reset. Both have been so helpful to me. Helps me stay connected, pay attention to what's going on around me, wake up, start again.

Light a Candle: I light a candle with one specific prayer or person in mind. Literally inviting light into darkness. The glow and pretty scent keep me prayerful all morning.

-WM

• • •

Walking Labyrinths: The path allows me space to surrender my burdens to God and receive His provision in exchange.

Daily Prayer: For nearly two years, a buddy and I have called each other five days a week and prayed for each other each morning.

-SES

• • •

Audio: Listening to 5-minute Lectio Divinas or spiritual words. Emily P. Freeman has a 5-minute audio Scripture and reading. I listen to this 2–3 times a week to center me. Her words, her tone, the music, and Scripture reading have been soothing and helping me begin again.

Stillness: Also sitting and looking for 15 seconds. Neuroscience says when you look at something for 15 seconds—it helps!

Movement: Yoga in my house. This adorable girl name Caroline Williams loves Jesus, uses Scripture, and has creative yoga moves on YouTube! So I don't have to leave my house!

Attending: One time a year I attend a class facilitated by a spiritual director. This past year I attended a three-week series on Love, Rest, and Joy.

Reading: Reading certain Bible stories, Christian books or magazines—helps me remember my faith! Stories, like *The Chronicles of Narnia* for example, help me hold on to wonder.

Cooking: Cooking! Baking! Gives me space and a place to be creative.

-KP

• • •

Orienting: I look around the space I am in (inside or outside) letting my eyes rest on anything that is pleasant to me or that I'm curious about. I stay with each thing for a bit (15 seconds or so) and explore what I like about it and how it feels in my body to focus on it.

-EH

• • •

Believing in Myself: When I work out, I feel massive connection to the fierce love in my soul and my own belief in myself increases. I can feel and sense God is close to me and even hear his voice more clearly in the moment. I can see which thoughts are not my own, which ones are, and which ones are straight from God.

-AP

• • •

Gratitude Journal: I started a gratitude journal after a conversation I had with a friend who had tragically lost her husband when her daughter was an infant. She was talking about how after her husband died, she felt like she regretfully missed a lot of the good stuff happening during that horrific time. She recommended simply taking note each day of anything good that happened. I have written everything from "unexpected extra income" to "surprise flowers" to "$3 off from Debbie's coupon at dinner!" Most are pretty short and I try to keep it next to my bed so I can jot down quick notes before I go to sleep. This helps me not only look back and see all of God's provision even amidst a hard season, but also reminds me to be present and aware in moments I might miss or forget otherwise.

Exercise: Running and yoga keep my mind connected to my body. Without physical activity I am a floating head that doesn't recognize what's happening in the rest of me.

The Meditation App, Headspace: Learning how to use meditation to become more mindful and compassionate in my response to the outer world has also yielded better sleep, less anxiety, better concentration, and a healthier approach to relationships.

The Beach: The beach feels like a space where I can breathe. And when I get my feet in the sand, I feel connected to myself and to God.

-KG

• • •

Checking In with My Body: Deliberately slowing down throughout the day and checking in to see what my body wants and needs.

-WB

• • •

Gratitude Practice: I used to journal gratitudes each morning. Now, I try to walk the beach in the mornings with my husband, and the first thing we say to each other when we get to the shoreline is, "So what are you grateful for this morning?"

Breathing: I have really appreciated deep breathing—breathing in the peace of Christ, exhaling worry, anxiety or fear.

On Assignment: I like to find quiet time to pray, focus on being attentive and getting my heart ready to be responsive. I sit still for a few minutes, and tell God that I am ready for an assignment for the day. What would He have me do? Who should I reach out to? What should I say? And then I make a list of what comes to mind.

Songs on Repeat: Over the last two years, I have had two songs in particular that have become my meditation and recentering songs. They are about 10 minutes long. I have listened to them on repeat, with my eyes closed, so many times that they instantly now bring me into a place of surrendering to God and waiting for Him.

-JW

● ● ●

Acknowledgments

If the only prayer you said was thank you, that would be enough.

Meister Eckhart

Thank you to the Christopher Ferebee Agency and the unwavering support of Chris Ferebee and Angela Scheff.

Thank you to my editor, Andrea Doering, whose wisdom and clarity always amaze me.

Thank you to Barb Barnes, who is a careful and thoughtful copyeditor.

Thank you to Brittany Miller, who has listened and translated all along the way.

Thank you to the entire team at Revell for their hard work, attention to detail, and care for this project.

Thank you to Shauna Niequist for her friendship, loving and generous support, and for lending her beautiful voice to this book.

Thank you to Emily P. Freeman, Trina McNeilly, Christy Purifoy, Mandy Arioto, and Kristen Strong, who read advanced copies
of the book and buoyed me with their affirmation and endorsement
of the project.

Thank you to the Norbertine Community of New Mexico for
granting me permission to reprint the exquisite poem by Fr. Francis
Doorf, O. Praem, that appears at the beginning of the book.

Thank you to the family and friends who were an abundant tribe
of cheerleaders during this project:

Melinda Miller, Eddy and Becky Miller, Bill and Joanie Tankersley, Lance and Laura Hatfield and family, Trey and Elyse Miller
and family, Peter and Jacquline Tankersley and family.

Ken and Elaine Hamilton, Jamie Rettig, Joanna Wasmuth, Tina
Rose, Linsey Wildey, Erica Ruse, Kate Jackson, Eric and Kara
Jung, Tatum Lehman, Corrie Klekowski, Debbie Cressey, Wanida
Maertz, Erik and Ashley Sorensen, Crystal Ellefsen, Krysta Hen-
ningsen, Jolynn Brown, Audi Swift, Katie Gardner, and Melanie
Connell.

Thank you to Beth Slevcove, who helps me listen with such
grace.

Thank you to Elaine Hamilton, Elyse Miller, Linsey Wildey, and
Crystal Ellefsen for reading and reflecting throughout the revision
process.

Thank you to those who contributed their wisdom and soul-
practices to the epilogue.

And, thank you to Steve, Luke, Lane, and Elle, who have each
helped me become more fully me. I love you. Always we begin
again.

Notes

Epigraph

[1]Francis Dorff, O. Praem., *Last Night I Died: Poems from Retirement* (self-published, 1999), 141. Reprinted with permission.

Chapter 1 On Opening Up

1. John 12:24–25.

Chapter 2 Held

1. Barbara Brown Taylor, *Learning to Walk in the Dark* (New York: HarperCollins, 2014), 129.
2. See Isa. 45:3 NKJV, NASB.
3. Ulrich Baer, *The Poet's Guide to Life: The Wisdom of Rilke* (New York: Modern Library, 2005), 15.
4. Gordon Hempton, "Silence and the Presence of Everything," On Being podcast, https://onbeing.org/programs/gordon-hempton-silence-and-the-presence-of-everything/.

Chapter 3 Donations for Those Less Fortunate

1. See Psalm 18:16–19 MSG.

Chapter 5 You Are the One You Have Been Waiting For

1. Charles Wesley, "Come, O Thou Traveler Unknown," *Hymns and Sacred Poems*, 1742.
2. June Jordan, "Poem for South African Women," *Directed by Desire: The Collected Poems of June Jordan* (Port Townsend, WA: Copper Canyon Press, 2007), 279.

Chapter 6 Let the Dead Trees Go

1. Parker Palmer, *Let Your Life Speak* (San Francisco: Jossey-Bass, 2000), 32.
2. Barbara Brown Taylor, *Home by Another Way* (Lanham: Cowley Publications, 1999), 50.

Chapter 7 You Weren't Consulted

1. Joan Chittister, *The Rule of Benedict: A Spirituality for the 21st Century* (New York: Crossroad, 2016), 188.

Chapter 8 Do Not Feed the Stray Cats

1. Richard Rohr, https://cac.org/change-catalyst-transformation-2016-06-30/.

Chapter 10 Bullying vs. Believing

1. Online Etymology Dictionary, s.v. "forgive," https://www.etymonline.com/word/forgive.

Chapter 11 A Threshold

1. Online Etymology Dictionary, s.v. "threshold," https://www.etymonline.com/word/threshold.
2. C. S. Lewis, *The Chronicles of Narnia: The Voyage of the Dawn Treader* (New York: HarperCollins, 1952).

Chapter 12 Bring Her to Me

1. See 2 Cor. 12:10.

Chapter 13 Love Is the Fuel

1. Isa. 43:2 NLT.
2. Isa. 43:3–4 NIV, emphasis added.

Chapter 14 This Is the Work We Are Doing

1. Heb. 9:15.
2. See Rom. 8:38–39.
3. Gal. 5:26.

Chapter 15 Speak Louder

1. See Matt. 25:14–25.
2. See Matt. 25:26–30.

Chapter 16 Around My Neck

1. See Prov. 3:3 NIV.
2. See Gen. 1:27.

Chapter 17 To Give Back

1. See Gen. 22.
2. Gen. 22:5, emphasis added.
3. Ps. 119:1.

Chapter 18 I Become Myself

1. Baer, *The Poet's Guide to Life*, 45.
2. Matt. 16:24–26.

Leeana Tankersley is the author of *Found Art, Breathing Room,* and *Brazen*, and holds English degrees from Liberty University and West Virginia University. Leeana's writing has been featured in *The Huffington Post*, cnn.com, incourage.com, and aholyexperience .com. She is a regular contributor to MOPS, both as a writer and speaker. Leeana speaks to groups all over the country about waking up those beautiful and sacred parts of each of us that can go dormant. She and her husband, Steve, live in San Diego, California, with their three kids. Learn more at www.leeanatankersley.com.

"Leeana says out loud the things we all feel, and she says them with grace and eloquence. Reading these pages is like sitting with a friend."

—*Shauna Niequist,* author of *Present Over Perfect*

"I wish I could get this book into the hands of every woman."
—*Ann Voskamp,*
author of *One Thousand Gifts*
and *The Broken Way*

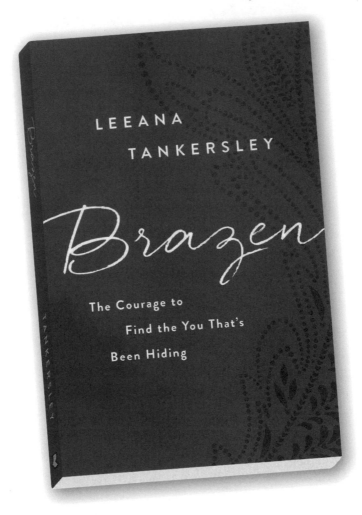

CONNECT WITH

Leeana Tankersley

at LeeanaTankersley.com

f tankersleyleeana

🐦 lmtankersley

📷 lmtankersley